IRON
TRIBE

IRON TRIBE

FROM GARAGE HOBBY
TO FITNESS FRANCHISE

DOING BUSINESS THE
IRON TRIBE WAY

FORREST WALDEN

Published by Advantage, Charleston, South Carolina.
Member of Advantage Media Group.

ADVANTAGE is a registered trademark and the Advantage colophon is a trademark of Advantage Media Group, Inc.

Printed in the United States of America.

ISBN: 978-1-59932-390-9
LCCN: 2013952354

This publication is designed to provide accurate and authoritative information in regard to the subject matter covered. It is sold with the understanding that the publisher is not engaged in rendering legal, accounting, or other professional services. If legal advice or other expert assistance is required, the services of a competent professional person should be sought.

Advantage Media Group is proud to be a part of the Tree Neutral® program. Tree Neutral offsets the number of trees consumed in the production and printing of this book by taking proactive steps such as planting trees in direct proportion to the number of trees used to print books. To learn more about Tree Neutral, please visit www.treeneutral.com. To learn more about Advantage's commitment to being a responsible steward of the environment, please visit www.advantagefamily.com/green

Advantage Media Group is a publisher of business, self-improvement, and professional development books and online learning. We help entrepreneurs, business leaders, and professionals share their Stories, Passion, and Knowledge to help others Learn & Grow. Do you have a manuscript or book idea that you would like us to consider for publishing? Please visit advantagefamily.com or call 1.866.775.1696.

THIS BOOK IS DEDICATED TO:

My amazing team at Iron Tribe Fitness, for helping me implement my vision, with greater speed and execution than I could ever have possibly dreamed. My coaches, managers, franchisees, partners, and executive team made this business fun and fulfilling to build, while helping me to keep the focus on changing others' lives in the process.

To my Mom, Marjean Brooks, for her tireless efforts in reading, rereading, and editing the finished product you hold in your hands. For my stepdad, Ricky Brooks, who has been the ultimate mentor for a young aspiring franchisor. To my Dad, Ken Walden, who taught me to believe in myself and in the power of affirmations at a critical time in my life.

Most of all, to my beautiful bride and best friend, Mendy. Without her love, support, and the unwavering belief in this crazy entrepreneur, there would be no Iron Tribe story to tell.

TABLE OF CONTENTS

It Takes a Team and We Are the Team

Capital Requirements

Site Selection: Location, Location, Location

Under Construction

The Learning Curve: Mine and Yours

You, Our Next Franchisee?

FOREWORD

Count me among the countless whose lives have been changed.

It all started one night when I looked at my wife and asked her, "Heather, how can I better love and serve you as your husband?" I was expecting her to at least have to ponder the question for a few minutes, so I was surprised when she responded with hardly any hesitation. Her words were piercing. "You can take better care of yourself," she said. "You don't sleep, you don't exercise, and you don't eat or drink healthy. If you don't take care of yourself, you're not going to be around (i.e., you're not even going to be alive) to love and serve me as my husband." At that moment, I realized that the way I was neglecting the care of my body was not just affecting me; it was affecting my wife, my family, and every other facet of my life.

It just so happened that a week later I was invited to "Bring-A-Friend Day" at Iron Tribe. I had heard about Iron Tribe, and Forrest had invited me on various occasions to try it out. I had successfully rejected his invitations before, but now that my wife had laid down the gauntlet, I knew I didn't have a choice, so Heather and I decided to go together.

Now when I hear "Bring-A-Friend Day," my mind immediately goes to nice, pleasant, "friendly" thoughts. I think of "friends" having fun together on a happy day. I must be honest, though; this "Bring-A-Friend Day" was neither fun nor happy for me. "A mere 12-minute workout," I remember thinking, "how tough can that be?" Little did I know that those 12 minutes (probably the longest 12 minutes of my life) would leave me lying on the floor with my legs threatening to explode. I could hear the hushed tones of people walking around me saying, "Is that guy okay?" A child of one of the members of the church I pastor came up to me and said, "Pastor David, you can preach a whole lot better than you can run." I wobbled out to the car and got in it with my wife. I looked at her and said, "That was miserable. Sign me up."

That was almost two years ago, and, simply put, I thank God for the transformation I have experienced on the journey that began that day. I thank God for the effect this journey has had not just on my physical health (which is night-and-day different than it was two years ago), but also on the health of my marriage, my family, and my life. I thank God for the community I have the opportunity to interact with every day—a community that continually challenges, encourages, builds up, sharpens, and supports one another. I thank God for coaches who not only provide instruction and encouragement for members as athletes, but who also show care and concern for members as people. I thank God for Forrest and others involved in leading Iron Tribe, and for the story you hold in your hands that represents his vision, passion, and determination. And most of all, I thank God that this story is not just about growing a business; it's about giving back to people here who deeply need greater health in their lives, and to people around the world who desperately need things like water to even have a chance at life.

Dr. David Platt

Senior Pastor, Church at Brook Hills

Best Selling Author of *Radical* and *Follow Me*

www.radical.net

3 – 2 – 1 GO!

t's Saturday at 7 a.m. and a tribe is on the move.

Groups of athletes at the downtown Iron Tribe gym warm up with push-ups, butt kicks, and jogging. As they stretch, they psyche each other up. They have come to prove that not only can they run a 5K, but that they can also do it after burpees, lunges, wall balls, and kettlebell swings. Many will run a course that includes steep, brutal hills. Competing in groups of three, their self-made t-shirts boast names such as "Kickin' Asphalt," "2 Eighty 3 Ladies," and "Call Me a Cab." Several franchisees have traveled to Birmingham, Alabama, bringing their own teams ready to compete.

The friendly "trash talk" flies across the room:

"Watch out, ol' man!"

"Time to put out or shut up…"

"I'll be seeing you at the finish line!"

The distance between three of the six Birmingham Iron Tribe gyms forms a loose triangular shape. Always looking for ways to challenge the athletes with competitive events, the Iron Tribe trainers created a three-man circuit race between these locations. "Tribefecta" was born in 2012—this year, 10 percent of more than 1,200 Birmingham clients signed up to compete.

Many have returned to the second annual Tribefecta in an attempt to better their performance from last year. With another year of training under their belt, they are confident and prepared for whatever will be thrown at them in the event; they will not know what's required until pre-race directions are given.

Luan, the event director, takes the microphone to go over the workout. He gives instructions for the movements, encourages good form, and provides strategy on emerging as the top team in the race. He describes the race route and informs the competitors that 30 Iron Tribe coaches are scattered throughout the course to help each team stay on track.

"Listen up! We're gonna find out how hard you've been working and what you've been eating! Make sure you sign in, know which leg you are in, and be ready five minutes before your heat."

A count-down clock is running, letting those in the first heat know when they should start. Warnings are given periodically. Anticipation grows with each announcement.

Tom, vice president of development, stands to the side with a franchisee prospect from New Jersey. A high-level investment banker, the prospect spent the last six months researching every fitness franchise organization in the nation. He believes Iron Tribe is the clear front-runner and wants to purchase the rights to most of the state of New Jersey, developing 30 gyms over the next 10 years. He turns to Tom and says, "I can't believe the energy and camaraderie you guys have created. This is unbelievable. I wish I could compete with them!"

Tom smiles. He knows that you have to experience the Iron Tribe community to truly understand it. Tom planned the franchisee prospect's trip around one of the weekend events so he could witness "up-front and personal" the culture they have been discussing on the phone.

Luan interrupts their conversation as he grabs the mic and sounds the final warning.

"Athletes in the first heat—one minute!"

"3 – 2 – 1 GO!"

Athletes with many different body types are competing today: young and old, male and female, runners and non-runners. They have trained for the past few months, enduring daily workouts at their respective Iron Tribe locations in order to be the best they can be and to prove it by successfully completing the course. Many will be vying for first place; others will be happy with a finish. Most are just excited to be accomplishing something they never thought possible when they initially stepped through our orange doors.

After completing the initial 10- to 15-minute workout, the competitors take off on the running portion of the event. The first leg travels roughly three miles from the downtown location to the original location in Homewood, which opened three years ago. Upon arriving at the Homewood location, the first athlete tags the second team member, who then begins the second workout and runs another three miles to the location in Mountain Brook. Occasionally, a van pulls alongside the runners as the creative team captures on video the agony and ecstasy of the competitors. Their banter is met with good-natured smiles and waves; the runners know the footage will likely end up on the weekly TribeVibeTV show. Other Iron Tribe coaches and supporters line the route to offer water and encouragement.

"You got this, man!'

"Keep it up!"

"You're doing great!"

One hour, 34 minutes and 53 seconds later, the first team member crosses the finish line back at the downtown location, completing the three-gym route. Entrance doors are flung wide open as Usher's "Yeah!" blares over the sound system. Spectators line the route and strain to glimpse the first contestants.

And the winners are… Cheers erupt, hearts pound, and backs are slapped in congratulations. Kudos are given to each competitor crossing the finish line, down to the very last one. Each considers himself a winner, no matter the time as he or she clocks in.

As the CEO, I am there to witness each competitor's finish. I greet Brant, who has been a member since the beginning, and congratulate him on his time. He responds, "Yet another successful Iron Tribe event, Forrest. I love this place and I'm in the best shape of my life."

I immediately reflect on a short time ago when a small group of friends were working out in my garage. Before the events. Before the corporate locations. And before the explosive franchise growth.

In three-and-a-half years, events such as Tribefecta have become commonplace in the Iron Tribe story—all originating from my little 400-sq-ft garage, which quickly expanded to six corporately owned gyms in Birmingham, and now includes an additional 51 franchisees in 10 other states!

How did this happen? Here is our story.

CHAPTER 1

MY FITNESS LOVE AFFAIR

I was the smallest guy on the football team in middle school. Not only was I the smallest, but I also had the double blessing of being the slowest! But I loved football and wanted to be a starter on the seventh-grade team. Therefore, even though I was terrified of the weight room, I forced myself to go every single day. I realized from an early age that my only hope of achieving athletic success would lie solely in my ability to outwork my teammates. In one of my first workouts, I remember getting pinned by 55 pounds in a bench-press attempt. That was not one of my finest moments. It was also a constant struggle to get stronger and put on muscle, but through sheer work and determination, I eventually became one of the strongest and fastest players on the high school team and experienced a great four-year athletic career. That began my lifelong love affair with working out.

When I graduated from high school and enrolled in Auburn University, I didn't know what I wanted to do with my life. I did know that I loved the physical aspects and challenges of working out, so I gravitated toward the study of exercise science. I became one of those rare people who never changed majors. The more I learned about performance and the human body, the more convinced I became that I was in exactly the right field. I didn't know *specifically* what I was going to do with my interest and passion, but I knew that whatever endeavor I chose had to be centered around exercise and helping others to transform their lives—the same way I had transformed mine.

AUBURN CHEERLEADING

I wanted to play on the Auburn University football team as long as I could remember. It was my lifelong dream to run through the tunnel onto the Jordan Hare football field as an Auburn Tiger. Although I received several scholarship offers from smaller schools, I never got the big offer from Auburn. I contemplated walking on the football team to realize my dream, but instead, I did the next best thing—tried out and made the Auburn cheerleading squad. We did everything the football players did, including running through that tunnel before the team. As an Auburn cheerleader, I was able to travel, receive a scholarship, and hang out with the best-looking girls on campus!

I realized the moment I was chosen that I was, again, the smallest man on the team. The strong muscular guys on the squad outweighed me by 35 pounds. That's when I took my dedication to the weight room to a whole new level. I began to set goals, keep a journal, and make things happen. I started devouring Arnold Schwarzenegger's books, identifying with the goal-setting techniques and positive affirmations he used and taught.

I'll never forget the summer before my sophomore year when, immediately after making the cheerleading squad, I bought a journal and wrote down my goal to be 30 pounds heavier by the time I set foot back on campus in August. Setting this specific goal made me feel powerful. That summer, I faithfully wrote down every workout and chronicled every meal or supplement I took. I chose not to join my friends who were partying every night. After four months of effort, I had put on 30 pounds of muscle. It changed my whole persona, my confidence level, and the way I projected myself. When I reported back to practice in August having achieved my goal, my sense of purpose was reinforced. I remember thinking to myself, "This is what I want to do with my life—help people achieve their goals the way I have achieved my own."

The confidence I gained was life changing, as I had always been shy growing up. The combination of performing as a cheerleader in front of 85,000 people and transforming my body started to change everything about me, including my personality. I even had the confidence to take the head cheerleader position and become the "mic man," leading the cheers over loudspeakers that projected to the entire stadium. I became extroverted. I felt empowered to talk to others, even offering my help when they were interested. I stepped out of my shyness comfort zone and began to engage with others with a sense of self-assurance. This transition defined my life, and further instilled the belief that you can change anything with hard work, discipline, and determination.

While I was on the cheerleading squad for three years, I was surrounded by amazing, motivated people who were going places with their lives. The association with my fellow cheerleaders saved me from the fraternity and partying scene, and placed me around strong Christians. They were serious about their studies (something I had not been, up to that point) and pushed me in many right directions. Even though dating another cheerleader was technically not allowed, I dated and later married Mendy, one of the girls on the squad. Thirteen years and four kids later, I'm sure glad we violated that rule!

All I have accomplished in my life, including this book, would not be possible without her constant support. She is an amazing wife and mother, one who completes me in every way—even in her own commitment to health and fitness.

30 Pounds Heavier and Holding my Future Wife in My Right Hand

NATURAL BODYBUILDING

As I gained muscle and studied fitness and nutrition, I wanted to find a way to be competitive. Although I loved working out, I missed the rivalry that came from playing football, so I decided to enter natural bodybuilding competitions. Knowing there was no way to compete with bodybuilders who were taking steroids (and not being willing to do that myself), I sought out and entered shows that included drug testing. I enjoyed the competition, and won many local contests.

I was still in college and training hard for bodybuilding competitions when people started asking me, "Man, how do you get in such great shape?" and "Could you help me do that?" Before I knew what was happening, I was in the personal training industry—I just wasn't charging money for it. I helped people because I loved working out and knew what it could do for them. At the same time, I was studying anatomy and physiology, my favorite classes in college. Not only did I love what I was learning, but I was also laying the foundation for what I would pursue my entire career. All the dots were connecting as a roadmap for my life began to emerge.

My First Bodybuilding Competition in College

It was interesting that none of my college professors could tell me how to make money from this passion for fitness and life transformation. All they said was, "Exercise science is a great major. It will enable you to find a job in corporate fitness or hospital wellness." But

I had no interest in either of those pursuits. I knew there had to be a different way.

PERSONAL TRAINING

I graduated from Auburn in 1998 and began a career in fitness. I worked in a local gym as a trainer and started looking for clients who were eager to change their lives. With no former business experience, my career was off to a slow start. However, my clients quickly began to see results, and this success helped me build an impressive client base. I also made good money for a young guy straight out of school. I was fired up! My strategies and coaching were changing people's lives and helping them to transform their bodies. But even as a 22-year-old, I realized I was not going to get rich working for a gym as a personal trainer. Although I was training 45 to 50 hours a week, I made money only when I trained a client in an hour-long session. I realized I was trading time for money, and working when everybody else wasn't. Since my clients worked out around their work schedules, most of my shifts were in the early morning, afternoon, and evening. Because I worked both ends of the day, I didn't see much of my new wife, who was an emergency room nurse at the time. This was not a formula for long-term success.

My mother remarried when I was in seventh grade. My stepfather, Ricky Brooks, is the CEO of Express Oil Change, a large automobile service chain. He often challenged me, "Forrest, what are you going to do with this love of exercise? How are you going to leverage it, make money, and build a career?" On the other hand, my dad, Ken, who had been a schoolteacher all his life, would say, "Get a good education and find a job that provides a reliable and secure career."

So one dad—the franchisor—challenged me to take my love for fitness to a new level by harnessing it and creating a business. My other dad—the schoolteacher—preached caution, security, and stability. Their conflicting advice and examples taught me valuable lessons and principles as each poured into my life through completely different perspectives. Later when I read the book *Rich Dad, Poor Dad* by Robert Kiyosaki, I thought, "Wow! I actually lived this book."

I had learned from *Rich Dad, Poor Dad* that creating leverage was the only way to build wealth and autonomy. I decided that continuing to trade my time for money was not sustainable, and started considering options that created leverage while still being involved in doing what I loved. How could I follow my heart's passion by building a true, sustainable business that was bigger than my talents and myself? My stepdad's words to me early in life were still ringing in my head.

Looking back now, I realize I was in what I call a "crisis of identification." For one thing, most people didn't consider what I was doing a real job. Back in the mid-to-late-1990s, personal training was not as prevalent as it is today. My friends were establishing careers as bankers, attorneys, doctors, and so forth, and I was the guy in the sweats at the gym. I couldn't escape the thought that maybe I did need to get a *real* job.

I evaluated other opportunities, and even considered working with my stepfather in his automotive-care franchise organization, as I would have a clear fast track with his company. But I just couldn't do it. It might be a good career, but I could never be passionate about changing someone's oil.

CHAPTER 2

GROWING THE BUSINESS

I decided to follow my heart and passion by opening my own personal training business. The problem was, I knew next to nothing about business and, because of lack of interest in the subject, hadn't studied it in school. I had simply lived and breathed fitness, for myself and others. Yet now I realized I lacked the skills to translate my passion into a true, sustainable, and scalable business that continued whether I was there to do the actual training or not.

Every time I dreamed about taking the next step and opening my own business, I was faced with questions I had no idea how to answer: How do I find a retail space and negotiate a lease? How should I structure the gym? Should it be membership-based or fee-based? Where do I begin? The questions seemed endless, and just when I thought I had answered all of them, more would take their place. I got so discouraged. Without knowing how to answer these questions and having no experience in opening a business, I couldn't get off the starting line. It was completely demoralizing and I wasn't sure what to do next.

One day, I found an advertisement for a franchise opportunity in personal training. I was surprised—up to that point I hadn't heard of franchising in the fitness industry. However, I had an intimate knowledge of franchising, as I had watched my stepfather build his own organization. This seemed like a perfect option for me.

The company was Fitness Together. I responded to the ad and flew to Colorado in February 2001 with Aaron Crocker, my business partner at the time. The franchisor, Rick Sikorski, picked us up in his Mercedes and took us to all the units currently operating in Denver. As he discussed the business model with us, he tried to sell me on the concept. Instead, I was focused on the type of equipment the gym had, and whether we would be allowed to customize it for the way we trained. I was thinking like a trainer instead of a business owner. Even though I wanted a scalable and replicable business in concept, I hadn't shifted my business paradigm beyond doing all of the training myself.

Finally, Rick stopped the car, looked me in the eyes, and asked, "Forrest, did you come here to talk about buying a business or did you come here to discuss equipment and training methodologies?" That moment was truly an eye opener that I will never forget as long as I live! It was clear I was thinking way too small, and it was time to create a new vision for myself. Although I still didn't completely understand the vital difference between being the personal trainer and the business owner, I did understand the question Rick asked. I slowly began to make the switch, looking at the opportunity through the lens of a business owner.

FROM TRAINER TO BUSINESS OWNER

The conversation with Rick began a major paradigm shift in how I viewed my role in building a business. About the same time, I read *The E-Myth* by Michael E. Gerber. Through this book, I learned I couldn't be the one doing all the personal training if I was going to build a successful business—I had to be the leader in growing the business, marketing the concept, and producing the sales. In other words, I had to be the one working *on* the business, not working *in* the business. Just because I was good at personal training did not mean that I was good at owning and operating a personal training business! In fact, I realized that being so well versed in the personal training side of the business could actually be a liability. It would be easy to focus only on the training and neglect all the other aspects of being a successful business owner that didn't come as naturally to me.

My stepfather agreed to co-sign a loan, which enabled me to purchase the Fitness Together franchise rights for the state of Alabama, including three locations in Birmingham. Since the gym I worked for was going out of business, I brokered the sale of the equipment for a commission, which covered the franchise fee.

I remember sitting in the banker's office with my carefully crafted business plan. Not only was she incredulous that anyone would ever pay the one-on-one rates we called for in the plan, but she actually said, "If Ricky wasn't sitting next to you right now, I would laugh you out of my office!" After negotiating the loan at the bank, but prior to the closing, Aaron, Ricky, and I stood on the bank's steps. My stepfather looked us in the eye and said seriously, "Guys, before you do this, understand—if my guarantee is called, Aaron, you will be out and Forrest will be working for me." His words only underscored the magnitude of what we were about to attempt.

Ricky didn't say it then, but later he told me he believed the franchise experience could be a great learning opportunity for my first attempt at business. In my mind, I was prepared for possible failure. I learned from Robert Kiyosaki, author of *Rich Dad, Poor Dad,* that while it is true only a few small businesses succeed, you have to be willing to start multiple businesses until you get it right! He said that FEAR stood for "Fail Early And Responsibly." Even with all these reality checks, I was eager to get started.

In June 2001, we opened our first location. Rick Sikorski flew down before our grand opening and took Aaron and me out to dinner. He laid a map of Birmingham on the table and told us exactly where and when we would open our next stores. "Here is where location number one will be, in six months you will open location number two, and six months later you will open location number three." Our eyes were as big as the dinner plates while we pondered the grand vision he cast before us. We believed we could achieve everything he outlined.

Rick Sikorski Attending Our Grand Opening

We opened the first location and experienced the best opening month in franchise history. We followed his incredibly aggressive plan of opening a new location every six months. Our goal was to dominate the market and we executed that plan, opening each location right on time. It was a circuitous and often-tumultuous path to success, which included a huge setback after September 11, 2001, when the world stopped. It seemed as if no one would ever pay for personal training again. Yet, we pushed through and enjoyed steady growth.

Aaron and I Racked Up 11 Franchise of the Month and 3 Franchisee of the Year trophies

In 2004, I purchased my partner's interest in the business and continued to grow the brand on my own. At that time, I had six studios in Birmingham. I also owned the rights to the state of Alabama and had others interested in franchising the model in my territory. I was excited about the potential growth of the concept. The Fitness Together model consisted of one-on-one personal training; each client had their own trainer and equipment in a private room. Each location had three to four separate rooms, depending on the size of the studio. Because personal training was just coming onto the scene, it was the right niche for the right time. The private room atmosphere appealed to customers who didn't want to go to a traditional gym, wait in line for equipment, or face the intimidation of the large "gym scene."

I thought the concept had tremendous growth potential and wanted to be a part of that future. Although I was experiencing amazing success in my six locations, including winning 11 "franchise of the month" trophies and three straight "franchise of the year" awards in Fitness Together, I was itching for the next opportunity to expand my business skills even further. My ultimate goal was to build passive income—a stream of income that flowed whether I was working or not. The realization of this goal started when I was 22, working with no leverage in my life, and reading *The E-Myth* and *Rich Dad, Poor Dad*. Now I began to see that being a master franchisee, managing a territory, and having franchisees under me would build the long-term passive income I longed for.

Once I made the decision to expand the business throughout the southeast, I sold the six studios I had developed, and bought as much territory as I could possibly afford. I added the states of Florida and North Carolina to my existing territory rights in Alabama. Then I put my head down, worked extremely hard, and over the next several years began the process of expanding the one-on-one personal training concept under the brand of Fitness Together. From 2005 to 2010, I sold and oversaw the development of 55 franchises in three states and became the number-one master franchisee in the entire company. I was realizing my dream of creating passive income while growing my business and leadership skills.

On a Support Trip to My Naples, FL Studio

My job description changed drastically when I focused on becoming a master franchisee. When I owned just six locations, I would stop in at my studios, work with my managers, and greet new clients. I was intimately involved in the product. As a master franchisee, I had a separate corporate office and limited direct involvement with the clients and the actual product of fitness. This change affected me more than I realized and set the stage for my growing discontent in my new role.

To hear more about what it took to become, not only the number-one franchisee but also the number-one master franchisee, go to **www.irontribefranchise.com/book.**

PASSION, IN A 400-SQ-FT GARAGE?

While building the Fitness Together business, my family had grown to include three young children, and my wife and I planned to add a fourth. I was traveling more than either Mendy or I had ever expected. Whether it was site selection, lease negotiation, or a support visit to work with franchisees on their marketing or staffing plans, it seemed like I was always on the road. I could feel myself losing my passion.

I couldn't put my finger on it. I was working in the fitness industry, building a successful business, and growing professionally. I had accomplished the goal of creating continuity and passive income, but I was enjoying what I was doing less and less. I had trouble understanding what was going on—wasn't this everything I had aspired to accomplish?

In late 2007, I started experimenting with CrossFit workouts. They were tremendously different from the bodybuilding workouts I had done up to that point. They wiped me out—just killed me. I enlisted a few friends to do the workouts with me and loved the group dynamic; it created an energy that intrigued me. Plus, the group workouts provided a new way to train and compete. Everyone performed the same workout and compared their scores—meaning I no longer had to participate in bodybuilding to satisfy my competitive urge. Now I could be challenged in my workout every day with my friends.

I enlisted my friends in this new endeavor, but we lacked a place to train. The workouts were difficult to do at the local gym. When I was kicked out of Gold's Gym for orchestrating a group workout, I decided to convert my 400-sq-ft garage into a gym. Before the conversion, I asked my wife if she minded. She said it would never last, but was okay with her as long as she could continue to park her car in the garage! Always supportive of my big dreams and visions, she had a practical side that balanced me at the same time.

I started with two long-time workout partners: one was a competitive bodybuilder, the other a competitive adventure racer. I knew they would grasp the concept of competitive high-intensity workouts. Like me, they were immediately drawn to the concept. We competed and challenged each other hard, and loved every minute of it. Our enthusiasm naturally spilled over to others, as we talked about it daily. I truly didn't expect what happened next. Suddenly, my neighbors wanted to join us, and then other friends who heard what we were doing wanted in. Eventually, my three-man test group grew into 17 friends—both my wife's and mine—who wanted to work out with us in our little garage gym experiment.

Top: The Original Garage Members
Bottom: All My Garage Workout Partners Gathered for My Birthday Workout

We worked out every single day and had an absolute blast! We hung out after the workouts, cooked healthy food, and enjoyed each other's company in a way that none of us had ever experienced in a gym setting. This created a fight club-like community in my backyard that attracted the attention of others. One day, Mendy said, "Look, we have more than fifteen friends working out in our garage and backyard. You've got to draw the line somewhere or this is going to get out of hand."

I didn't charge anyone to come, nor was I trying to make money. In order to have a competitive atmosphere, I simply needed others to work out with me. I had no plan or desire at that point to start a new business. I was having fun rediscovering my passion and getting extremely fit. I still traveled to all my territories and supported my franchisees. But I was seeing a tremendous shift in the industry—away from one-on-one personal training toward group fitness and semi-private training—one trainer working with as many as four clients.

I was witnessing the future of the industry in my garage. Because of peer pressure, people were pushing themselves harder than they ever would have with a personal trainer—they didn't want to be beaten by a friend or quit in front of the group. I also realized that competition was something that appealed to everyone. If I could find a way to get others to experience it, they would be hooked in the same way my little garage band was.

Teaching Others My New Passion

To see clips of the early garage gym workouts, and to hear further commentary about the early days, go to **www.irontribefranchise.com/book**.

CHAPTER 3

CHANGE IS BREWING

While I was excited about my garage gym experiment, I was losing heart over the travel and job responsibilities necessary to build a master franchise company. I vividly remember thinking to myself one sweltering morning after completing my garage workout, "How is it that the best part of my day is spent in a small, unairconditioned garage?" I realized I was dreading the start of my day and going to work, a dilemma I had never experienced before.

To complicate matters, as I visited my franchisees, I didn't see the kind of results and testimonials that I saw from the participants in my garage as they changed their lives. We had guys who had never worked out or played high school sports dropping 40 pounds, meeting personal records on their 5k runs, and starting to care about how much they could deadlift. These things were completely foreign to them before they stepped foot in the garage.

At the same time, most of my clients who paid top-dollar for a private, personal training service weren't making many changes at all. They weren't losing much weight, could care less about being competitive, and were only there because they felt they should be or their doctor had prescribed exercise. Of course, we had some great clients who grasped the concept and had jaw-dropping results, but I couldn't figure out why they seemed to be so few and far between. For almost two years, a thought simmered in the back of my mind, "Man, if I could start over, I would create something totally different, something based on what I experienced in my 400-sq-ft garage." Finally, I went to the CEO of Fitness Together and told him I wanted to go in a different direction by pursuing a group fitness model. He said they were committed to a one-on-one based model, but would love to have my territory back! After much soul searching, I sold all my territory to the corporate office, a move that enabled me to create something new from scratch.

It turned out to be the biggest decision of my life.

THE TURNING POINT

I wrestled with it, prayed over it, and lost sleep over it. I had accomplished everything I had set out to do by building an amazing organization with 55 franchisees. The money was great and led to a comfortable lifestyle for my family. We lived in our preferred neighborhood and drove the cars of our choice. Was it worth jeopardizing everything on a new venture? Could this little garage gym experiment really be the future, replacing everything I had already built? Or was it a phase I would always regret?

From the beginning, Mendy was completely behind me making the change. I told her, "You've gotten used to a comfortable lifestyle. This will be like starting all over again, and may be a tremendous risk. That means my name will be back on leases and bank loans, and we probably won't have a salary for a while. Are you prepared for all of that again? Do you remember how many hours I poured into the business in those early years?"

I'll never forget the conversation we had on a dinner date. I launched into my whole starting-over spiel Mendy had heard a million times by this point. She stopped me and said, "Forrest, you *have* to do this. You're not the same man you were when you started with Fitness Together. You're not as excited. You're not as passionate. I'm behind you one hundred percent. I know you'll make it successful. You've got to do it."

Mendy Has Always Been My Greatest Fan

That sealed the deal. Even when the risk was high, having a wife who believed in me meant everything. Mendy gave the final confidence to follow my passion and build the business of my dreams.

PASSION FUELS MY PURPOSE

In the midst of losing passion for my career, I had started traveling internationally on mission trips. The pastor of my church, David Platt, challenged us to spend two percent of our year, or seven days, on an overseas mission trip. I accepted the challenge and traveled with my dad to Tegucigalpa, Honduras, in summer 2007. While there, I experienced another defining moment.

I stood in the middle of a dump, watching the people who called it "home." A pregnant woman walked in front of me, dragging a trash bag while battling birds and cows as she searched for the most edible thing for her next meal. My mind flashed to Mendy, who was at home and pregnant, as well. Their circumstances could not have been further apart. I couldn't decide which was worse—that the poor woman's baby had been conceived in the dump or that it was going to be born in the dump.

I thought about everything I had acquired up to that point—the vacation home at the beach, the BMW, the businesses that were opening and running successfully—and I had one of those "God moments." I felt He clearly spoke to me saying, *"Forrest, what are you going to do with your time, talents, and treasure? It has to be something bigger than yourself."*

Processing the Honduras Dump Situation

That question led to deep soul searching. I realized I had lived in a "bubble" my entire life and truly hadn't understood how most of the world lived. The next year, I took trips to India and Sudan and my world opened up even further. I witnessed true poverty and learned the stark reality that most of the world lived on less than two dollars a day. I saw the same problem in every place I traveled—the lack of clean drinking water. In Sudan, I visited kids in a hospital who were dying from diarrhea and other water-born diseases so easily cured in America. As I walked through that poor dirty hospital, praying at the bedside of dying children, I couldn't let myself envision for even a second one of my children in those beds, or I would have completely broken down in front of the kids and their families. Among the many factors that cause illness and poverty, it appeared that lack of access to clean drinking water—a basic human necessity—was one of the main reasons the poor suffered. Up to that point, available clean water was something I had taken for granted. I had never considered the millions in the world who had no access to it, and how that lack affected every single detail of their lives.

I felt called to do something about what I had witnessed on these trips. So along with my two good friends, Spencer Sutton and Mark Whitehead, we created the non-profit ministry Neverthirst (www.neverthirstwater.org). The ministry's vision is to bring clean water to the poor through the local church. Since the start of the ministry in 2008, we've been blessed to be able to raise more than $5 million dollars and develop 1,500 water projects, which serve roughly 200,000 people in Asia and Africa. Neverthirst digs deep-water wells, provides filtration systems, and offers hygiene education in South Sudan, India, Central Africa Republic, and Cambodia. Everything is coordinated through the local church, which increases its ministry and allows them to share the good news—providing not only *physical water* but also the *living water* found in Jesus Christ.

Through observing the poor and their living conditions, I gained tremendous perspective about my life and the resources we have in America. For a time after this experience, I thought I was called to devote all my time to the ministry, travel the world, and work on behalf of the poor. It was clear to me that the water crisis was massive and that I could spend the rest of my life helping to ease the suffering of the poor. Was this the reason I was losing my passion for business, because God was calling me to build a ministry instead? After I saw children dying from a basic need for clean water, how could I do anything else with my time, effort, and focus? Through prayer, fasting, and journaling, I came to the conclusion God had given me talents in other areas for a reason. The excitement I felt about the garage gym and starting a new business was the very gifting, passion, and desire He would use to benefit others. As I became more and more certain that starting over and creating a new fitness business was my calling, it became obvious that I needed to connect the fitness business and Neverthirst by using the same platform of a successful business to impact the poor and marginalized around the world.

One of over 80 Wells that Iron Tribe has Built With Neverthirst

God used a verse from Scripture to confirm this. Psalm 67:1-2 (NIV), begins, "May God be gracious to us and bless us and make His face shine on us." Everyone loves that part because we want the blessings. We agree by saying, "Yes, God, please bless me." Up to this point, I had focused on the blessings but had disconnected them from the purpose. The second part of the verse says, "So that Your ways may be known on earth, Your salvation among all nations." There is a purpose to the blessing!

Through this process of building a ministry, I've learned we have a responsibility to be a conduit of God's blessings. Yes, we should pray for blessings, manage our money as good stewards, and grow our business, but then we should also hold these things with open hands and use them to bless others the way He's blessed us.

This life lesson has led to many changes in my life. First, Mendy and I were led to seek international adoption, and in May 2010 we adopted a child from Ethiopia. Benjamin is a healthy, thriving toddler who has been a wonderful blessing to our family. The desire to adopt and rescue him from a life of poverty came from our travels with the ministry. We saw the plight of the orphans as we visited orphanages, and witnessed children dying in hospitals. Then we came home, looked at our house, and said, "We have room. We have resources. Why not adopt one of those children and give him a forever family and a future?"

Meeting Benjamin for the First Time

Second, it led me to create a business that was about more than just me—more than a workout, more than a gym—but instead about an entire community focused on changing the world. It has been amazing to see how our clients have embraced causes that are important to us and how thankful they are to be offered ways to give and be involved in issues that truly matter!

The entire Walden family

To see clips of those early Neverthirst days and to hear further commentary from me and the other cofounders, go to **www.irontribefranchise.com/book.**

CHAPTER 4

A TRIBE IS BORN

I'm constantly asked, "How did you come up with the name?" The answer stemmed from those early days in my garage. We developed a reputation around my city as "the cult in Forrest's backyard." We were a tight group—excited about what we were doing and the huge improvements we were making in our fitness.

I wrestled with the word "cult" because it had such a negative connotation and was contrary to my Christian upbringing. I tried to think of a positive word for a tight group of people. I played around with the word "tribe" and, because we were in Birmingham, which is known as the "Iron City," I added "iron." We were lifting iron in the gym, after all. And that's where "Iron Tribe Fitness" came from. I thought it was perfect, because it explained who we were and what we do: we're a group of committed individuals who work out together and collectively make each other better.

When I finally decided to turn the underground garage gym experience into a business, I knew I wanted to do it right where I lived—in Homewood, a suburb of Birmingham. To build a commercial environment similar to the garage experience, I would have to create a brand, an experience, and a facility that would be attractive and inviting to all kinds of people.

GETTING IT RIGHT . . . FROM THE BEGINNING

I decided to spend the same amount of money on design, brand, and aesthetics as I did on the equipment, furniture, and normal amenities a gym requires. I didn't want the concept to be too hardcore or aggressive for people in mainstream America. Not only were they the ones who could afford our group-training services, but they were also the ones who needed it the most. If I was going to address the obesity crisis in Alabama, the second fattest state in the nation, I knew I had to reach the average person, and not cater to a small percentage of elite athletes. Although I started the business as a CrossFit affiliate, I quickly realized our goals did not match those of the CrossFit movement. We de-affiliated and continued the process of developing our own brand and concept.

From the beginning, I wanted Iron Tribe to become a franchise business. Every decision regarding the website, equipment package, or layout for the gym was filtered through the question: "Can this decision be replicated in hundreds of locations?" If it couldn't, I threw it out, and if it could, I fine-tuned and tested it. Sometimes it worked. Sometimes it didn't. I fully embraced the *E-Myth* concept I mentioned earlier—building a scalable model that could be duplicated in hundreds of locations.

But first, I had to have a working prototype. I had to prove that my concept could deliver everything it promised. The first location in Homewood became my test kitchen. Initially, I was one of the coaches. Of course, I hired staff to work with me, but I wanted to experience the product firsthand with clients to make sure all my assumptions were correct. Plus, I had so much fun being back in the day-to-day functions of a fitness business that I was eager to start working directly with clients again! I coached for the first three months, then moved to the manager position and got off the floor. I stayed in that location three more months before hiring Luan Nguyen, an associate since 2002, to take over. I backed out of day-to-day operations in order to focus on opening the next location.

It was incredibly confirming to watch my vision become reality, and to witness the impact it had on both clients and staff. At the end of a long shift of training, a client told me how thankful he was that we had opened Iron Tribe and described the ways his life had changed. Not only were his comments great to hear, but they also affirmed my passion of helping clients to improve their lives through fitness. His words also validated that I was doing exactly what I was created to do. Here was proof that the business worked and would continue to work with all types of people. Clients as young as 6 and as old as 70 were embracing the workouts, altering habits, and experiencing transformational change.

Something different was going on here. As a one-on-one personal trainer for 15 years, I had done everything in my power to keep clients engaged and motivated. But the goals they set were mostly appearance-based outcomes: "I want to lose 20 pounds," "My daughter's wedding is coming up and I need to fit into my dress," or "The doctor said I need to lower my cholesterol." Whatever the goal, more often than not, it was something related to their physique.

These goals were not powerful or immediate enough, in most cases, to modify behavior. Losing 20 pounds or lowering cholesterol was not sufficient motivation for someone to put down the beer or pizza at night. The goals did not compel people to make the lifestyle changes necessary to achieve results. Also, in the dynamic of the one-on-one training environment, clients often became comfortable with their trainer, didn't continue to push themselves hard, and sometimes even questioned the exercise being prescribed. In other words, one-on-one training was not affecting the change I thought it should, which frustrated both me and the client.

Iron Tribe offered a different option—a group dynamic coupled with competition. This dimension added motivation for clients to reach the next level, while being rewarded for their effort. Hundreds of years ago, Napoleon said, "Men will die for ribbons." I found this to be true in our program; rewards tap into an innate part of human behavior. Men (and women) will "die" (work out as hard as they possibly know how) for rewards. They'll die for points, die to better their performance by seconds, die for taking a spot on the leaderboard, die for winning the workout, and die for posting the top score on our app or website. The amount of effort clients exerted in the group setting could never have been realized in years of one-on-one training.

I learned not to talk about personal aesthetics. When customers began our program, instead of putting on the body fat calipers, weighing and measuring, and doing all the things I had done before, I told them to focus on performing like an athlete by becoming faster and stronger. Once they grasped the mentality of an athlete and participated in training like one, the results came. This competitive dynamic was powerful in modifying behavior, whereas the aesthetic and health goals were not. For example, when a guy lost in competition to his buddies, came in last in the class, or a was beaten by a female (which I saw happen all the time), all of a sudden he cleaned up his diet or stopped the nightly glass of wine or bowl of ice cream.

When a client ate horribly over the weekend and then saw how his or her performance suffered the next day, suddenly it clicked: "Oh my gosh. How I eat, how I sleep … it really does relate to my performance in the gym." The connection with his or her behavior outside the gym and the performance inside it changed everything; suddenly they worked to improve both, and succeeded.

I threw the conventional fitness wisdom out the window: instead of making the result the goal, I concentrated on developing athletes. The results came, almost as a side effect. That's really the key to the whole program. By setting up an environment where the customer is competitive and able to excel, they accomplish so much more in life—not only in the workouts, but also at home, at work, and with the family. And when a customer succeeds, everyone wins. The client gets results. In return, we receive renewals, referrals, and the joy of helping people change their lives in the process.

SELLING OUT . . . AND AT THE RIGHT PRICE

Because the business was growing quickly, I was able to market at a higher price point, almost double that of most competitors in my city, by blending the benefits of one-on-one personal training into a group environment. By the economy of scale, I charged less than the going rate for one-on-one personal training, while at the same time commanding a premium price for group training. This allowed me to market aggressively, build a staff with full-time benefits and career opportunities, and provide a service that people readily embraced.

We set a very aggressive goal—enrolling 200 clients in our first six months—and hit it to the day. I didn't know who our clients would be in the beginning, but they turned out to be professionals, business owners, and stay-at-home moms; basically the same type of clients that I had seen in the one-on-one personal training world. These clients experienced fitness that was fun, hard, and competitive, while also being less expensive than paying a one-on-one personal trainer. At an average of $250 per month, we were more expensive than a single membership to a fitness center, but the price was a third to a half of the cost of hiring a personal trainer. We were perfectly positioned to capture a segment of the market that was not being served by the low- and high-end fitness offerings.

The Original Homewood Location

I knew I had a model that worked. It worked for the clients—they got amazing results. It worked for the employees—they developed careers they were passionate about while truly helping people. It worked for the owner—we served the members, hired and retained top talent, and built a very profitable business at the same time. I had moved through the system, from coach to manager, but then it was time to take myself out altogether. I had to prove that the business could be duplicated across multiple locations if I was going to build a successful franchise model. My initial goal was to open eight gyms working independently of me in different areas of Birmingham. I didn't want people to point to that first store in Homewood and say, "Well, of course you were successful. You started it. You were coaching and your friends from the garage came."

CHAPTER 5

THE FRANCHISE PROTOTYPE

I n June 2010, one of my clients, Jim Cavale, sat down with me and wrote his own position contract. "Forrest, you should hire me for your corporate office. I see what you're doing, I'm experiencing it as a client, and I love the model. I'm passionate about it and I want to help you build this business to the level we both know is possible." Jim has never had a problem seeing or believing in the huge vision I had for Iron Tribe. I looked the contract over and said, "Well, Jim, that's great, but I don't have a corporate office. In fact, the next thing I'm doing is opening a second location. If you're willing to start at the bottom and work your way up through every position, then I will consider letting you open our second store. If that goes well, then maybe we can discuss a future in the corporate office helping me build the franchise organization."

Me and Jim Cavale

Jim eagerly agreed. He started as a coach, obtained his certification, coached classes, and quickly moved into management at my existing store. He opened the second store in January 2011. We always considered that second location the franchise prototype—the kind of easily duplicated model we thought would work in "Anytown, USA." It *had to* work anywhere if we were going to be successful. For this reason, we opened the store in a strip mall. I didn't want interested franchisees to walk into the original Homewood store in the old renovated building and think, "I've got to have this unique building in this cool little downtown area to make it work."

The second store was deliberately placed in a strip mall on Highway 280 in a busy suburb of Birmingham. This location forced us to develop an architecture plan and design an equipment package to fit the empty 3,400-sq-ft site. We took a raw strip mall space and turned it into an incredibly attractive Iron Tribe gym. Every market in America had a strip mall; this conversion demonstrated the scalability of the model.

The Franchise Prototype Located in a Strip Center

The Finished and Scalable Product

I also wanted this store to be the pure franchise prototype without my personal involvement. From the beginning, I've never coached a class there. I didn't sell a client. I didn't manage the location. Jim was in charge from the beginning, operating the store, effectively acting as our future franchisees would when opening and operating their businesses. In fact, in the first two weeks the gym opened, I was in Ethiopia adopting my son Benjamin, and Jim was at the 280 location executing the business model.

All of our competitors, and even some of our clients, said, "This will never work on Highway 280." The area was not as community-focused as Homewood. Plus, there were three competitors within a half-mile radius who offered a group-training program and charged half our fee. From those very first locations, we had "haters" who predicted we would fail because we expanded too fast, marketed too much, and were overpriced or too "professional." I learned if you don't have people talking negatively about you, then you just aren't doing enough. Negativity goes with the territory.

The haters believed the Homewood location worked because of my participation and reputation, and because it was in my own backyard. So it was really satisfying to build the new store on Highway 280, and not only build another thriving tribe, but to quickly grow it to maximum membership capacity. Yet, more exciting than proving the doubters wrong were the testimonials pouring in from our members. Our clients were experiencing amazing results, and I was receiving stories of transformations like I had never seen in my career. I immediately told my staff, "The second these types of results and testimonials stop, we are focused on the wrong things at the corporate office and the store level!"

At the first store In Homewood, we sold out the available 200 memberships, and then extended the limit to 250, and eventually to 300. Once we hit the 200-client mark, we realized we had additional capacity in our classes, and started offering more classes in a day than we had originally anticipated. This allowed us to work with more clients, while still giving them a great experience and continuing to serve them well. We eventually capped the limit at 300, because growing any larger decreased our ability to engage with every member and create the close community that drove our entire model. This was completely opposite from the regular fitness model, which signs up as many people as possible, hoping they don't come. Our model created desire and a sense of urgency, because clients knew there was a limited number of memberships. Once we sold out, we stopped offering them. Once we maxed out, we created a waiting list that indicated it might be months before an opening was available. By limiting the growth to 300 members, we knew everyone's name. We knew their goals and their reasons for coming. They became like family to us, and the clients knew they were not "just another number." We cared whether they showed up or not, and were fully invested in each person experiencing great results from our program.

PROOF OF CONCEPT

We had another winner in the Highway 280 location. Just like Homewood, the quick growth began with an amazing team who were fully invested in our mission and vision. It was exciting to demonstrate that our system worked and could be reproduced. From the beginning, I told my staff that Iron Tribe provided the potential for developing a successful career path. If they were great employees, embraced our core values, and continued to learn, they would be able to advance in the organization. Even in the interview process, I painted a picture of moving from part-time to full-time coach and from full-time coach to manager. With my vision of developing eight corporately owned stores in Birmingham, and ultimately growing into a franchise organization, they could possibly own their very own Iron Tribe Fitness (ITF) gym! I'm not sure how many of my employees believed my vision in those early days, but any doubt soon faded as the second store became reality, and they were offered the option of moving to the new location and eventually into management.

The Staff was Growing and Buying Into the Vision

I pulled Jim out of the second store in May 2011 to act as head of operations, since he had proven himself as an operator by building the store to more than 100 athletes in less than four months. This allowed us to promote other staff members to his position, fulfilling my former promises. Then we laid the groundwork for more locations as well as our franchise office, and started the process of franchising the model. Not only had we proved that our model was scalable and worked successfully in multiple locations and different geographic areas, but we also opened more of our own stores while consistently growing the existing ones. As owners, we have always aspired to be the best operators in the system, setting the bar for all our future franchisees while challenging them to beat us at our own game.

In June 2011, we rented a little 400-square-foot office, which we affectionately named "Global," and started to build the franchise model. The first step involved creating the federal disclosure document (FDD) and filing it with the Federal Trade Commission. Then we designed an operations manual and checklist, and created a video-based membership site, which would equip our managers and franchisees with tools and videos on every aspect of implementing the model. We knew that both time and money had to be invested in building the technology that would create a consistent experience and ensure all our stores operated exactly the same way, every time. We could not find a single off-the-shelf system that provided the desired automation and regulation. So we began the arduous and expensive task of building our own websites, apps, and software to run our systems and business model.

In order to accomplish this, I freed myself from the daily operation of the stores and handed them over to Jim. As chief operations officer (COO), Jim oversaw each of our corporate stores, which gave me the ability to focus on the franchise model, prepare to sell to new markets, and support our franchisees. That was not an easy transition for me—I love operations and had a fear of being too far from the product again, like I had been with my previous business. Jim not only developed tools that allowed me to keep my finger on the pulse at the store level, but he also was able to help me grow the next phase of our business. This change in responsibilities turned out to be crucial, because I needed all the extra time I could manage to get the business to the point that it was ready to be franchised. I knew it would be a ton of work, but I couldn't believe how much had to be thought through, built, and systematized to realize the goal.

I was so thankful for my relationship with God that kept me centered, and for my daily workouts in the gym that provided a natural outlet for goal setting and positive affirmations. Every time I felt overwhelmed or defeated, I simply took a five-minute walk from Global to the Homewood gym, grabbed a workout, or visited with clients and staff. Immediately, the passion for what I was doing would come right back. I felt I had a distinct advantage over other business owners because I was surrounded by a highly motivated staff, and clients who were working toward their goals in a positive environment while they were getting in the best shape of their lives. The Iron Tribe environment, which pushed others to work as hard as they could and challenged them to believe they could accomplish the impossible, kept the CEO motivated, as well. Although there were hard days in the process, we persevered and built the franchise company while continuing to develop our corporate stores.

For some clips of those early days at the 280 gym, the Global office, and commentary from Jim on taking the leap to join Iron Tribe, go to **www.irontribefranchise.com/book**.

MORE SUCCESSFUL LOCATIONS . . . AND
A THRIVING CORPORATE OFFICE

In searching for our third and fourth locations, I was adamant about one location being connected to the corporate office. I didn't want to get too far from the product again—I had made that mistake in the past. Since I'm a fitness guy at heart, I needed to continually be involved with the clients as they transformed their lives. That is what keeps me passionate and I never wanted to lose that motivation again!

We found an old dilapidated warehouse/office building in downtown Birmingham, which we purchased and built into our third location—a beautiful 3,500-sq-ft gym next door to 2,500 sq ft of space for our corporate office. Again, the naysayers said, "It will never work in a downtown environment. You guys are growing too fast. This whole thing is going to collapse on you. You will never be able to sustain this rapid growth!" I took that as a challenge and did everything in my power to prove them wrong once again.

The Downtown Location with the Corporate Office Attached

We opened the downtown store in March 2012, and had an amazing start. Luan moved from the Homewood location to take charge of growing the new gym. Just like the other stores, this third addition had more than 200 clients within the first six months. We equipped the franchise office and started hiring people on the franchise side. Just as the nearness of "Global" next door to the Homewood location had kept me plugged into what was going on, having the corporate office next door to our new location kept me motivated. I could walk next door anytime, grab a workout, go through a class, or talk to some clients. Even when I was in meetings or on the phone, I could hear the thumps of weightlifting next door, or see groups of clients running past my window. Those glimpses would give me the extra burst of energy required in a fast-growth startup. Many times, I would find myself at my desk working on something that I didn't particularly enjoy, like a pro forma or endless paper work. All I had to do was go next door and talk to clients or watch a class, and it juiced me back up. Then I could return to my project and knock it out with passion!

While developing the downtown location, I also bought a beautiful building in a desirable neighborhood called Mountain Brook, which is considered the "old money" section of Birmingham. This building housed an existing personal training business, and was a perfect location for one of our stores. In fact, it was the only location that would work in this area of town. I had been keeping my eye on it since launching Iron Tribe. When the building went on the market, I jumped on it. Even though I had just purchased and developed the downtown building, I was so confident in our model that I decided to go all-in and take whatever risks necessary to grow the brand. The Mountain Brook gym opened in April 2012, bringing our store total to four locations. We had an absolutely amazing reception from the Mountain Brook community and signed up more than 65 clients within a month. Everyone had heard about us coming to town; their friends were giving us rave reviews from their experience at one of

ITF Mountain Brook

our other three locations. All the stores were growing like wildfire, and we were having a blast. The third and fourth stores benefited from the first two stores doing well, as they generated great referrals. The town buzzed about Iron Tribe—our unique marketing left an impression. Potential clients saw how fanatical our members were, the results they were getting, and how much they loved it. It seemed everybody wanted to know about the Tribe!

Since we were growing so fast, we were careful to stay in control of the growth and the model. We remained absolutely focused on creating the systems and processes that would ensure a consistent experience for our clients at each and every location. We knew these systems needed to be implemented and executed by the average operator, and not require superstars to perform them. We wanted standardization at every level—site selection, equipment package, facility, and coaching consistency in the daily workout in every class at all locations.

I was convinced the primary possible drawback to our growth would be a lack in my own personal development and that of my team. So I invested in multiple mastermind groups, such as a Vistage CEO coaching group, Strategic Coach, and a high-level marketing mastermind group led by one of my business mentors, Dan Kennedy. I also asked a former colleague, Tom DeLosa, to join our team as vice president of development. Tom and I had worked together closely for 10 years in Fitness Together—he was my development support rep when I developed and later sold my 55 locations throughout the southeast. He had left Fitness Together and was heading up the sales team for an adult care franchise organization in Denver. Although he was doing extremely well in his position, he missed fitness and was struggling with his passion, just as I had been. Even though we had no franchise sales yet, I was so confident about the direction we were heading that I made an aggressive offer to bring Tom and his family all the way from Denver to join our team in Birmingham. I had seen Tom's character and work ethic first-hand, and believed he had the perfect DNA for helping us shape the future of ITF. Tom had been watching our growth and was so excited about what was going on he approached me about becoming our first franchisee in Denver. I told him I would love that, but I would rather him come to help me build the franchise company in Birmingham. As soon as I made the offer, he jumped at the chance to get back into the fitness business. He quickly sold his house, purchased a new home in Birmingham, loaded his family in his RV, and made the 1,300-mile trip south! I was amazed to see him take such bold action based on my offer, and was a bit nervous about hiring a senior-level executive without having sold a single franchise!

With a growing franchise office, four thriving locations, and more than 1,000 happy clients in Birmingham, profits starting to roll in and we continued our plan of market domination. After carefully searching and negotiating real estate, we found two locations that opened simultaneously in early 2013. The first was a 5,000-sq-ft space on the end-cap of a strip mall in Hoover, Alabama, which we completely renovated. It was initially in such poor shape that I had to spend more money in renovation than I had ever spent before, but I knew the area justified everything I was pouring into this location. At the same time, I purchased a 7,850-sq-ft building three miles down the road that served another part of Hoover on Highway 150. This was another one of the "dream buildings" that I had been watching from the inception of the brand. After staying on the market for more than two years, the owners finally reduced the asking price to a realistic range. I was able to work out a 2,000-sq-ft sublease with another company, and we set out to build our nicest location yet. Both locations began growing rapidly. As of the writing of this book, they are on target to accomplish the same success that the other locations have experienced.

To prepare for the rapid expansion planned for the first quarter of 2013, we increased our staff to 25 coaches and managers. We brought in top-level talent and trained them within our system while they waited for their opportunity to grow into leadership roles in the two new stores. We used the existing four locations to train new staff so they were quickly brought up to speed and were ready to step in to operate the new stores from day one. The two new locations are off to an amazing start and the sky truly is the limit in what we can do with this model in Birmingham, and beyond!

The Staff Continues to Grow

FINALIZING THE FRANCHISE MODEL

With six locations operating in the Birmingham market after three years, we were well on our way to the initial goal of building eight stores in less than five years. That is an average of two corporate stores per year, and we anticipate opening the next two in 2014 as we continue to grow and maximize our current locations.

One of my primary goals was to have multiple stores in a single market. To accomplish this, I created a prototype to establish an effective business model that could be duplicated and scaled across multiple geographic areas and demographics; it wasn't a "one-shot wonder." I proved, through multiple locations, that the business could run independently, and wasn't only about me, my personality, or my experience in the industry. Finally, I had to show serious investors what developing a geographic area, and achieving economy of scale through staffing and marketing, could accomplish. If one location was too small for an investment, we could provide a larger-scale investment with the benefits of multiple locations and promotion of the brand.

The prototype proved that not only do we sell and believe in this model, but we also execute it with excellence every day. One of our guiding principles is to be an operations-based culture—everything we do, any system we build, or any marketing plan we initiate has been perfected in our own gyms. We've tested it. We've tweaked it. We've refined each element, making sure it worked before adding it to our system and passing it on to our franchisees. We're not an ivory-tower corporate office with little connection to the real world experience, or merely developers coming up with plans and marketing campaigns in a vacuum. We're actually testing each improvement in our own stores every day.

I believe this is a key differentiator and a large part of our success. I've never wanted to create a culture in which the corporate office doesn't operate stores. Otherwise, there could be great disparity between what the franchisee experiences in day-to-day operations and in what the corporate office thinks is reality.

In our operations-based culture, almost everyone in our corporate office has direct experience as a coach, manager, or both. This means that most employees a franchisee encounters know and understand the model; they are not just "hired guns," so to speak. They have been in a gym setting, working 12-hour days, signing up and servicing customers, and doing everything within their power to execute the model—just like we are asking our franchisees to do.

Developing six stores in Birmingham, while simultaneously building our franchise system, has been a great learning experience. It has forced us to make sure we are documenting systems, creating steps that can be duplicated, and designing technology and systems that are replicable in hundreds of locations. We have demonstrated that all procedures can be executed with high quality, value, and return on investment to the operator. Running these two parallel paths in the developmental process was extremely valuable, as our initial assumptions and plans didn't always work. Many times, we had to go back to correct miscalculations, update information, or improve tactics.

One of the greatest tools in this analysis process has been surveying our members. We have figured out what works best for our customers by asking them what they wanted. For example, we carry our own prepared meals and snack line because our members told us, "We buy into the diet that you're teaching, but we're having a hard time implementing it or finding the time to prepare and cook it every day."

We constantly ask our clients and ourselves, "Are clients getting value every single time they come in for a class? Do they realize value every time their debit card gets hit for monthly membership? How can we continue to create value on a day-to-day basis?" If our clients ever leave our doors thinking, "I could have done that on my own," or, "Nobody even knew I came today or called me by name," they will be not be renewing their contract, and the value proposition is lost forever. The most important part of the entire system is creating an experience where this never happens, and passing this knowledge on to franchisees.

Many of the tweaks, programs, and classes we've offered also have come from asking our employees what we needed to address. Our staff is on the floor every single day, interacting with our members. In monthly meetings, an open forum allows staff members to report areas that need to be changed or addressed. Surveys also provide a way for our trainers to give written feedback on the model in a more immediate manner, allowing them to directly affect the decisions we make. And, because client testimonials continue to be the litmus test of our success, their responses tell us if we are delivering on our promises or not. Are we providing the best possible experience and changing lives? That's where the rubber meets the road.

One of my favorite books regarding a startup business is *Pour Your Heart into It* by Howard Schultz. He positioned Starbucks not as a commodity—just a place to get a cup of coffee and that's the end of it—but as something greater. He noticed how fragmented our society had become without a central gathering spot for people to interact, and he imagined each Starbucks location becoming "The

Third Place." Because everyone had separate work and home environments, he positioned the Starbucks model as an additional venue for people to gather.

That's what Iron Tribe is creating—a sense of community that is absent in our clients' lives. When competition, improvements in fitness, and increased energy are additional benefits to gathering in that place, an entirely different level is achieved. It becomes an integral part of our members' support system—one they didn't even realize was missing. Even though Starbucks has built a powerful gathering place, I think we have an opportunity to create an even more compelling "Third Place" that truly changes people's lives. Judging from the hundreds of testimonials we've received that testify to life transformation, not just physical change, I would say we are well on our way!

ULTIMATE MARKETERS OF THE YEAR

In February 2012, I learned that Infusionsoft, our customer relationship management software of choice, was about to hold their annual conference. Even though we had used the system for less than a year, I told Jim Cavale (who was VP of operations at the time) we should apply for the ultimate marketer contest during *InfusionCon*. Not only had we accomplished unique things with their software, but we had also realized amazing results. (Later in the book I will discuss this major aspect of our technology.)

We applied by documenting our system-wide changes and highlighted the incredible results since implementing their software. After reviewing all applicants, Infusionsoft's board selected the four contestants who would compete on stage at the conference for the title of "Ultimate Marketer of the Year." Viewing previous winners and their businesses on the website convinced us that this was a prestigious award, which, if received, could propel us to new levels.

We were selected as one of the four, which meant we would be competing at *InfusionCon* in Phoenix on April 2, 2012. The date was an interesting coincidence—it was the same day our fourth gym opened, and also the day we had picked to launch our franchise model!

During the conference presentation, Jim and I shared our story about the growth of the Iron Tribe business, the success with Infusionsoft, and the process of leveraging the software to supercharge our model. After hearing each of the four finalists present their stories, the 1,500 business owners in attendance (who also used the software) voted on the winner. We were up against some tough competition from three business owners who had experienced fantastic growth in the previous year. After all the votes were tallied, Jim and I were crowned the *Ultimate Marketers of the Year*! I think our story resonated with attendees because of our passion for what we were doing and the lives that were being changed. This was evident through the use of great technology, client involvement in the program, and life-changing testimonials, many of which we shared from the stage.

Those factors, along with the scalability of our efforts, and the speed with which we were accomplishing the results, ultimately led us to be crowned the winners.

Being Announced as The Ultimate Marketers of the Year

There we were, on stage in Phoenix, with our fourth store opening that day in Birmingham. This was just more confirmation the business worked apart from our direct involvement due to the automation and scalability capacity we had generated with Infusionsoft, other proprietary technology, and our detailed systems. It also confirmed that our model was ready for the next step of franchising, and we promised the full-capacity crowd we would be back in a year to report results from the franchise model.

The national recognition accompanying the award opened numerous doors for us. Infusionsoft sent us to seven cities on a speaking tour. For the rest of the year, we shared our story and worked with other business owners. We described the process of leveraging marketing and online media, plus the process of converting leads to customers, and nurturing customers once they got started.

It proved to be an invaluable experience, and one that sharpened our public-speaking skills. We went to New York, Chicago, and

Jim and I Excited to See Our Brand in Times Square

California multiple times, giving our brand great exposure. We met many others who were building and growing businesses, and are leaders in their respective fields. Infusionsoft loved our story and what we had accomplished, especially the 300 percent growth year-to-year. In fact, they liked it so much that they sent a videographer to Birmingham to document our success, and then flew us to New York.

Infusionsoft rented a huge billboard, revealing the short documentary they had prepared about Iron Tribe, and then interviewed Jim and me afterward regarding the impact of our brand and our goals for the future. Those few days were a tremendous media event, and propelled our story and brand into the public eye. Imagine our amazement as we stood on 42nd Street and Broadway, watching the Iron Tribe story on the Jumbo-tron in the middle of Times Square! We were written up in the *Wall Street Journal* and several other national outlets, and were selected as *CRM* magazine's elite company. Multiple articles were published about us at home in Birmingham, and everyone was talking about our business. You just couldn't buy that kind of buzz if you tried!

To see the keynote presentation that won the title of Ultimate Marketers of the Year, as well as the short video that Infusionsoft put together and played in Times Square, go to **www.irontribefranchise.com/book.**

LAUNCHING THE FRANCHISE BUSINESS

The time had come. Momentum from the Ultimate Marketer award, along with the fact that we had replicated our prototype multiple times while refining our systems, led us to eagerly and confidently launch our franchise model for sale in April 2012. We set an aggressive goal: sell 10 locations in the last eight months of 2012. We reached out to all our existing clients, letting them know we were ready to discuss the franchise model, and presented them with an opportunity to partner with us by opening their own Iron Tribe location in the market of their choice. We had no way of knowing the overwhelming response we were about to receive from our current clients! It was the ultimate vote of confidence. Our clients showed a passionate interest in the brand we were building, which propelled many of them to become part of expanding throughout the nation.

Most of the clients who responded were successful business owners or professionals with great existing careers. It was both surprising and encouraging when they told us, "I love what you've built. I love it as customer. Iron Tribe changed my life, my family's lives, and I want to be a part of it." That was a typical response.

Every client who was interested in franchising completed a multiple-step process that involved webinars, calls with VP of Development Tom Delosa, and due diligence on their part and ours. If they were still interested and qualified, they were invited to join us for "Discovery Day," where franchise prospects got an in-depth look at ITF. They were shown the Iron Tribe opportunity in full—the systematization behind the business model, as well as the culture, marketing, software, technology, and tools. Because they had experienced it as clients, they knew firsthand we had delivered on our promises and had created a remarkable experience. What they didn't realize as customers was what happened in the background to allow the stores to be operated so seamlessly. Once they saw all the tools, technology, systems, and videos, they realized how much had been going on behind the scenes. They could easily take the model and replicate it, because we had done the hard work of creating, documenting, and building a proven and repeatable system.

Toward the end of the book *The E-Myth,* readers are encouraged to envision presenting their system to a potential buyer. In this exercise, we were to pave the road for a sale by showing every component working flawlessly, whether we were physically present or not. Exhibiting our model at Discovery Day gave me the ultimate satisfaction that we had, indeed, created an incredible system that was ready to be replicated, and had the potential to bring immense value to our brand partners!

Discovery Day also allowed us to engage in mutual evaluation. We had more opportunity to appraise the clients and decide if they were the type of business owners and operators we wanted as franchisees. The clients could, at the same time, evaluate us and ask themselves, "Are these the kind of guys I want to work with while building my own business?"

Most of the first clients who went through the process wanted to open stores in Birmingham, but we had already decided not to sell franchise locations in our area. Although that turned away several clients who were initially interested in franchising, we knew it was the right long-term decision. We wanted to keep Birmingham as a corporate market, ultimately with eight locations that will lead the entire system in sales. We always want to be the number-one operator of our own system!

Once they understood that Birmingham wasn't available, we helped interested clients identify multiple cities and locations that were perfect matches for our model. We began to sell franchise locations left and right. Client investment groups followed my exact prototype by investing in Multiple Development Agreements (MDAs) that allowed them to reserve up to five territories in their desired city. We initially grew in the southeast almost in concentric circles—out to Tuscaloosa, Montgomery, Mobile, Auburn, Huntsville, Nashville, Chattanooga, Knoxville, Charlotte, Raleigh, and Atlanta—all great markets around Birmingham where the model fits demographically.

By the end of 2012, with the first eight months of franchising under our belt, we had not only exceeded our goal of 10 franchise expansions, but had absolutely crushed it to the tune of 29 locations sold! As excited as we were about the growth, we were even more encouraged by the caliber of franchisees who would become our brand ambassadors. Of the 29 locations we sold that first year, only one of the owners had not previously been a client. That particular franchisee was a vendor who wanted to know why we were selling more of their product than anyone else in the world. Curious about what we were doing, he and his team went through the sales process and were invited to Discovery Day. They were so impressed that they decided to invest in their own franchise location. Being directly involved in our industry and servicing gyms across the country, they recognized we had a special product and system, and wanted to be part of it.

Our very first franchisee's story epitomizes the success we desire for everyone who becomes part of our brand. Richard Martens lived the typical personal trainer lifestyle: working a full-time job in real estate while coaching fitness classes on the side. He never thought he could make a living from his passion for fitness, and had resigned himself to use it as a hobby. As he watched us sell out our first location in Homewood, and then announce plans to open the second, he jumped at the opportunity to see if we could deliver on our promises. He began coaching at Iron Tribe part-time, quickly moved to full-time, and eventually managed our Highway 280 store when Jim was promoted in 2011. Because of his confidence in the model, he partnered with his brother, Will Martens (also an ITF client), and together they purchased four locations in Nashville. Within two years of joining our team, Richard had quit his job in real estate, built a career in an industry that he loved, and become a business owner following his passion! I love how that story shows career opportunity: the right employees are able to see the potential, experience the model, and consequently invest by opening their own stores. Today, Richard and Will have a thriving location in Brentwood, Tennessee, and are not only building their second location, but are anticipating adding even more locations than the initial four in Tennessee and Mississippi. This kind of proven success with our staff-turned-franchisee allows us to continue to attract top-notch talent—those who are eager to join our team and become the next success story.

The initial franchise growth and momentum resulted from a spillover of product excellence; as people recognized the impact Iron Tribe had on their lives, they wanted to be involved in providing the same benefit for others. It has been rewarding to experience tremendous *internal* growth from those who know us best—our clients. Now we're generating significant *external* interest; others are witnessing our fast growth through national press. Individuals who have never had the customer experience are finding us on the web and beginning to inquire. Because of this, expansion didn't slow down in 2013, and franchise sales are continuing to pour in.

We were given the opportunity to speak again at *Infusioncon* 2013, and to share what we'd done since winning the 2012 award. This year, there were 2,400 business owners in attendance to hear our story. We shared the stage with influential speakers such as Daymond John from Shark Tank. In our keynote presentation, we reflected on a year before that—when we had just opened our fourth location but hadn't sold a single franchise. That was then. Now we were on the same stage, not only talking about our six thriving corporate stores, but also the 32 franchise locations sold up to that point! By any measure, this was massive growth that was due, in no small part, to the automation and technology provided by Infusionsoft, in which we have continued to invest. Many people were blown away by the presentation of our accomplishments over such a short period of time—we actually ended up selling five locations from that one keynote speech!

Giving Away the Ultimate Marketing Title in 2013

To watch the *Infusioncon* keynote presentation from March 2013, go to **www.irontribefranchise.com/book**.

Our initial goal for the franchise company was: 100 units open in three years, and 300 units open in five years. With 51 locations sold after only 15 months of franchising, we are actually ahead of that aggressive goal. We are more confident than ever in the Iron Tribe brand and believe we will have the opportunity to expand this system to thousands of units.

Although we have received international interest, an extended market is not our focus now, and won't be for a long time. In fact, we have already turned down requests to open stores in California, because we don't want to grow that far west too quickly. In a recent franchise sale of three locations in Denver, Colorado, became the dividing line for expansion in the next year. I've continued to receive inquiries from the West Coast and have had conversations with people in Australia, Africa, and—believe it or not—even the Middle East.

FRANCHISEES PROVE THE MODEL

One of the most exciting parts of this journey has been watching our initial franchisees take our business model and execute it well, while impacting clients' lives at the same time. Introducing a new group of clients to Iron Tribe, and watching the systems work in brand new markets is an amazing experience. As of this writing, we have nine locations open: two in Nashville; and one each in Montgomery and Huntsville, Alabama; Raleigh and Charlotte, North Carolina; Johns Creek, Georgia; Chattanooga, Tennessee; and Naples, Florida. We have an additional 15 locations underway in different phases of site selection, lease negotiation, or construction. The just-opened locations are off to an awesome start, and we are already starting to see proof that we can, in fact, reproduce the culture and DNA of the business model created in Birmingham. In several instances, our franchisees are accomplishing their goals better and faster than we have. For example, our Belle Meade franchisee in Nashville set the all-time opening record for pre-sales, completely shattering anything corporate has achieved in Birmingham. They also tied our record in reaching the 100-client milestone.

As proud as I am about client growth, I am more thrilled about the potential expansion of the Iron Tribe culture. Original garage member and now franchisee Jamie Warren confirmed this when he called late one night. He said, "I have just returned from attending an event at my gym in Nashville. Clients were thanking me for bringing this business to their city. They were passionate and excited about the results they were getting. They love the great team around them, and told me how much Iron Tribe had impacted their lives. I felt like you must have felt for the last few years, when Birmingham clients gave you that same feedback!" I immediately thanked Jamie for sharing this encouragement. Here was proof that, not only was the business model able to be reproduced, but also the culture, core values, *and* the right team!

CORE VALUES

As the founder of the brand, I was deeply involved in formulating Iron Tribe's vision, mission, and goals. It was critical that our core values be identified and developed from the beginning. What guiding principles would characterize the business? Against what grid would we weigh our actions and make decisions? I felt this aspect would be crucial to our success as we conducted business every day based on established core values.

Early in the start-up process, I blocked out a few hours at a local coffee shop to study an article by Jim Collins on vision, mission, core values, and goals. I was putting the finishing touches on the Iron Tribe vision when Jim Cavale (who was just a client at the time) came up and asked what I was studying. I gave him a copy of the *Harvard Business Review* article and told him he should be developing the same concept for his business. Little did I know that our simple conversation about core values would plant a vision in Jim's mind to do everything in his power to sell his current business and join mine!

Our number one core value is: Excellence in everything we do. The pursuit of excellence was the reason I was ready to sell my existing business and start all over again in 2010. If this business wasn't about excellence in every aspect, then I wanted no part of it. Excellence is paramount—at the coaching level, in a class environment, in teaching a basic movement like the air squat, in a weekend event, in the franchise office, or on a Discovery Day when we present the business model to potential franchisees. We continue to challenge ourselves, holding each other accountable to perform every action with utmost excellence. This is not always easy, and it takes constant vigilance. Often, it means facing the brutal fact that we are not living up to an incredibly high standard in one aspect or another of the business. However, knowing this is the standard—and that nothing else will suffice—leads us to correct the areas that are coming up short, and to continue to push the business toward excellence.

The number two core value is: Live the code. If we're going to ask our clients to work out intensely, use functional movements, and eat a specific diet, then we have to lead by example. For instance, we don't want our clients to see staff out at a restaurant having beer and pizza on the weekends. We must be the leaders in the same lifestyle we are promoting and selling. This is hiring and firing criteria for Iron Tribe. I've interviewed individuals who wanted to work here but couldn't get past the requirement of having to be serious about the lifestyle we teach. It doesn't mean we're 100 percent perfect, but our leadership and staff must consistently practice right behaviors. Congruency in this area is paramount to our belief in, and selling of, fitness each and every day to our clients.

Working Out Together After a Staff Meeting

The third core value is: Honesty and integrity. Most people respond, "That goes without saying. Of course, you're going to be honest and have integrity." But many opportunities present temptations to cut corners, hedge on the truth, or compromise integrity. This could happen in a situation between members of the team and me, or with a client. It could occur with a vendor who possibly forgot to bill us or billed the wrong amount. Are we going to sweep it under the rug, or are we going to be honest and do what's right? As leaders, we must be willing to be honest with ourselves by examining whether the business is living up to its brand promises and core values. Promoting honesty and integrity permeates our team meetings, individual reviews, client committees, coaches' committees, and surveys. We hold ourselves accountable to this core value, and attempt to live it out each and every day.

The fourth core value is: Giving back. This is based on Psalm 67:1-2 (quoted earlier). As we have built this business, we've been able to connect the blessing of success with charitable causes, not only in America, but also around the world. We've created two annual fundraisers that have become bigger than simply Iron Tribe initiatives. One of those is WOD (Workout of the Day) for Warriors. Once a year, we participate in a workout that raises money for wounded warriors through an organization called Team Red, White, and Blue. The first time we sponsored this event, we raised $25,000 for the troops, and created a WOD for Warriors movement.

The movement built greater momentum in the second year. By raising money through their workouts, clients enabled us to contribute more than $35,000. Mike Erwin, a West Point graduate and the founder of Team Red, White, and Blue, took note of what we were doing and approached us about packaging the program and offering it to fitness facilities nationwide. This year, there were more than 200 fitness facilities running the WOD for Warriors program with us. We raised $50,000 in Birmingham alone, and hundreds of thousands of dollars were raised across the country! The event was birthed through a desire to bless others. Our nation's warriors need more help than anyone I can think of, as they often come back wounded and beaten down. This issue is dear to Mendy and my hearts. As I write this, my brother-in-law, an Army Ranger, just returned home from Afghanistan. I see the struggles and sacrifices his family makes to protect our freedom, and know that he has seen more than his fair share of soldiers coming home wounded or dead.

Mike Erwin of Team Red, White, and Blue has involved Tim Hasselbeck (Indianapolis Colts quarterback in the NFL) and his wife, Elisabeth, along with several other high-profile people who love what we're doing. Mike and his organization provide up to 10 memberships for veterans at each ITF location across the country. Because of the success of the WOD for Warriors movement, Mike has decided to move their functional fitness camp (formerly held in Washington, DC) to Birmingham. Iron Tribe will be in charge of running the three-day event, drawing veterans from all 50 states.

We've Raised Over $110,000 for Team Red, White and Blue

We also created WOD for Water, which benefits Neverthirst (the non-profit I co-founded to help build water wells in India, Africa, and the Central Africa Republic). Once a year, we focus on the world's water crisis and challenge our tribe to participate in, donate to, and find sponsors for a fundraiser workout. We've run three WOD for Water events and raised $145,000 through those! Last year's event alone raised more than $100,000. That money goes straight to areas where clean drinking water makes a huge difference in people's lives.

A connection has been made between our tribe here in Birmingham and tribes in Africa and India. We've been able to share photos and reports of what our members have helped accomplish, telling them, "This is what this village looked like before they had access to clean water, and because of you, this is what happened afterwards." They've been able to watch interviews with village women who used to spend hours walking to retrieve water. Now, because of easy access to clean water, they use that time to make a living for their families, and are able to send their kids to school.

WOD for Water has Become a National Success

This is transformational for their communities, and connecting our ITF community with others around the world is powerful, as well. This year, for the first time, we're taking a trip to India with several of our Iron Tribe members to show them the 40 wells that were dug with the money from the last WOD for Water fundraiser. They will witness firsthand the work being done through Neverthirst and the local church. All these benefits are the result of connecting the blessing of the business with the greater purpose of what we feel we're called to do. And it's a direct response to the challenge I received in the dump in Honduras, when I was asked how I would use my time, talents, and treasure to count for something more than myself.

The fifth core value, and probably my favorite one, is: Hard work and continual self-improvement. The Iron Tribe executive team and I are all devoted to self-improvement. We continually read books, listen to audio programs, attend events, and participate in mastermind groups. I think one key to growing a business is to grow personally. At the same time, we challenge our staff, franchisees, and even our members to invest in their own education. Many nights, I'm at one of the locations or filming a webinar until 10 p.m., teaching a goal-setting workshop for our members. This is more than just a gym; we are teaching people how to take control of their lives and improve them, one step at a time. Doing the extra hard work is not easy, or every business owner would be doing it. Steve Jobs once said: "You have to have a lot of passion for what you do, because if you don't, any rational person would give up." The goal of excellence demands hard work; our passion motivates us to get it right and deliver more than promised.

The employees who have grown the most in our business are the ones who've been serious about this core value. They often come to me and ask, "Forrest, what books would you recommend?" I make suggestions; they read the book, come back with questions, and ask for the next recommendation. This interest has led us to establish a library at the corporate office, which is accessible to all staff. On our website, there is also a special section directing interested followers to books we are currently reading and studying. Staff members who don't want to read, but who would prefer to sit at home playing Xbox on the weekends, are the ones who remain in the same position and probably aren't a good long-term fit for the team.

We do everything in our power to live out the core values on a daily basis. I am always on the lookout for employees who live the core values, and compliment them on their efforts in front of the team. I challenge the staff to take ownership of the values, and to see them as more than just a list of suggestions.

Living out the core values directly affects our business. We believe our actions attract the right staff and clients who—although they don't see core values plastered on the walls or in our advertising—get a feel for who we are. They sense we're authentic, and grasp the fact that we are about much more than fitness. We attract like-minded individuals, and I think that's the reason we've been so successful in our fundraisers. We have the privilege to work with like-minded people who share our core values and want to give back as part of their experience.

CHAPTER 6

THE IRON TRIBE PROGRAM AND WHY IT WORKS

B y now, you are probably wondering what differentiates our program from every other fitness concept out there. The difference is the client experience, and that is what we sell every single time a client walks into an Iron Tribe location. Because we have a "high-touch service" rather than a physical product, it requires the staff and coaches to live the brand and operate out of our core values. This aspect creates a dynamic experience each and every day for our athletes. We must over-deliver value at every workout so the client never leaves thinking, "I can do this on my own now that I know and understand the movements."

Another contributing factor are the workouts themselves, which are generated at the corporate office. Every client at every location, whether corporately owned or franchised, does the same workout on the same day. Each unique workout is created by our coaches committee, which is overseen by Director of Training Luan Nguyen. Luan is also responsible for coaching, and developing the coaches. Reflecting the requirement for corporate staff to have operations experience, he first managed several locations. Luan has been overseeing creation of the workouts since day one, and has accumulated more than 1,000 that work perfectly with our space and equipment package. The coaches committee, which consists of one of the top coaches from each corporate location, makes sure each workout is standardized. They also set the standards for scaling the movements and workouts so that every single client can customize the workouts to their capacity and fitness level. This allows a wide range of clients, who may be at completely different fitness levels, to compete against each other in an identical workout. Not only does Luan oversee this committee, but he also stays updated in many fitness certifications, which enables Iron Tribe to keep a pulse on what is new. Through this exposure, he is able to develop tools that equip our coaches and help us stay on the cutting edge of the industry.

In the daily workout, we emphasize functional movements, or movements that we do naturally as a human being. We use very few machines. Instead, we focus on using our own body weight in movements with rowers, pull-up bars, and jump ropes; and using external weight, such as barbells, kettle bells, and medicine balls. We focus on common physical movements clients have used since childhood. We include exercises such as bear crawls, broad jumps, jumping jacks, push-ups, squats, rope climbs, and pull-ups. We also emphasize movements like dead lifts, or lifting a bar off the ground to waist height. This is one of the most functional movements because, as humans, we are constantly picking things up. Or we use an overhead press with a barbell, which correlates to something as simple as putting luggage above your head in the overhead compartment on a plane. Everything we do translates to real-life situations and building more strength to perform them.

A Downtown Class enjoying a Run

Most people who exercise traditionally do so by themselves, going through the same routine of walking on a treadmill or doing a certain number of repetitions with weights for chest, triceps, or biceps. Even in a typical bodybuilding program, the workout is boring, done in isolation, and doesn't produce great results for the average client. They simply move from machine to machine, and often end up in a rut.

Initially, people are surprised at the lack of machines in our gyms, and there is a very specific reason for their absence: most machines do not relate to how your body naturally moves, so they have very limited results. For example, when a person grabs the handles on a chest fly to perform the motion of bringing their hands together and squeezing the chest, he or she is performing a dysfunc-tional movement. It locks them into an isolated movement pattern that they were never really intended to have. In other words, the movements don't translate to real-life situations and don't provide improved fitness capacity.

Functional movements, on the other hand, are not only incred-ibly effective, but they are also safe, because they mimic the natural movements of the body. Add to functional movements a constantly changing program and there is no room for boredom—clients never know what they're going to get! The workout may include a basic gymnastic movement, weight lifting, and a run, all in the same period. Or, it may be a weight-lifting-only day. This flexible and changeable workout program keeps everyone on his or her toes; all must adapt to whatever gets thrown at them as they walk in the door. It also creates a high degree of anticipation and fosters the client's desire to workout more frequently than they ever have in their life!

The program is incredibly effective, because the body is constantly recovering from the stress of different types of workouts. Each day brings a challenge, which prevents working out becoming boring and routine. A client is learning a different skill and doing it in a distinct format. Not only is it fun, but it also encourages creativity, learning, and embracing new things. Many clients take their "can-do" attitude outside the gym by enjoying novel experiences such as mountain biking, running in a 5K, water skiing, rock climbing, or other activities they have never tried before. Since achieving an increased fitness capacity, they have fresh excitement in applying it elsewhere in their life.

Compare this to the experience in the regular gym scene, where a person is alone doing a routine he or she saw in a magazine. They are often just walking from machine to machine—there's no intensity. They are not working hard, not trying to set a personal record, and not competing with anyone. No one even knows they're there, and the staff probably doesn't know their name. This just breeds complacency, boredom, lack of results, and a very high attrition rate.

When you walk in our gyms, everyone is doing the same workout. You know exactly what your previous time was in the same workout, or you can look at the board and see who's had the best time that day. Now you're competing to try to either beat your own time or beat somebody else's time, and to possibly have the best time for the day. It creates a positive and competitive environment.

All components are working together to maximize results and efficiency. You're using movements that are safe and effective, you're varying it in ways so that it never gets boring, and you're in a competitive environment that creates results never seen before. It creates what I call "stickiness." People stick around—they are constantly talking about the workout, and they actually *want* to do it. They say, "Man, this is the first time I've really looked forward to going to the gym. I've never seen results like this."

Having spent so many years in one-on-one personal training, the difference between the two models astounded me. In personal training, although people pay top dollar and receive great instruction, the desired results weren't being achieved. Most of the time, the thing people initially signed up for, they just didn't get. And, after six to eight weeks in the one-on-one environment, I found that my staff's role became more like therapist than coach. They spent so much time in conversation that clients would invariably start talking about their lives, asking for advice and opinions. I taught my staff to say, "Let's get back to the workout."

Because of the group environment, this does not happen in our model. There are two full-time coaches and a maximum of 20 clients per class, which doesn't allow for one-on-one interaction. Instead, what is fostered is peer-to-peer accountability, which I have found to be far more powerful! Of course, the coaches are there, overseeing the whole dynamic—correcting form and coaching intensity in movement. The only focus is, "We're going to get in here, we're going to work hard, and we're going to get it done." The clients are in and out quickly, with more effort and sweat in a short amount of time than anything they have ever done.

Every session lasts 45 minutes, including the warm-up, workout, and cool down. Our clients come three to six times a week; the frequency depends on the their budgets, goals, and schedules. Once a store is sold out and fully staffed, we offer 12 to 14 classes a day, with several programs to choose from. The clients choose from any of the workout times in any of our local gyms. They can even schedule a workout online or on their smartphone through the Iron Tribe app.

After completing a workout, the coaches record a client's score. Although we create a competitive group environment, the real competition is often the clients competing against themselves. When they first begin the program, their first response often is to focus on beating their previous score. As they progress, they begin to compete with others in their class, eventually with others in the gym, and then with those working out in different locations.

The scores are posted on an acrylic wall that we call "the leaderboard." After each workout, they are also posted on our website and in our iPhone app, so members can see how their score compares to others. An ESPN-style ticker scrolls across the top of the website to keep everyone updated with the leaders of the day.

This creates an amazing dynamic; an accountant sitting in his office can compare his score with an attorney buddy across town as they talk about it on our website or on Facebook. It gives our clients the competitive outlet they had while playing sports in high school and college. For most of us, other than running the occasional 5K or playing on a recreational softball team, there's no sense of daily competition in our lives anymore. Iron Tribe reawakens the competitive spirit.

After a client has been involved in the program for two to three months, I often hear the comment, "I haven't felt like this since..." They continue by filling in the blank with whatever was the hardest and most structured activity they've ever done. "I haven't felt like this since boot camp in the Marines," or "since high school football," and even "since band camp." The group workout experience brings them right back to that moment. Tony Robbins, a motivational speaker, self-help author, and life coach, says that you are a direct reflection of the expectations of your peer group. This couldn't be more true at Iron Tribe! Not only are clients pushing themselves harder than they ever have before, but they are doing it with a group of like-minded teammates who expect them to finish the workout and work their hardest while doing it. This is life changing for many.

CHANGING LIVES

The results we see are dramatic. Our clients are reminded that they can be passionate about life by setting goals and achieving them. Their excitement and enthusiasm about their success invariably spills over into every aspect of their lives. Because we have seen this spillover repeated consistently, we know the change we are effecting is much bigger than just fitness. Fitness is our tool, but it is often simply a catalyst for improvement in all areas of peoples' lives. It's common now for people to tell me they've lost 50 pounds—it hardly even surprises me anymore. If clients had lost 50 pounds in my one-on-one days, I would have done back flips and made them my poster child!

Lately, we have received several hundred pound-plus weight-loss testimonials, which is exciting. A whole new group of people who never thought that they could do this type of program have experienced life-changing results. However, even more exciting than the weight-loss stories are the ones about clients using their newfound fitness success as a catalyst to change other areas of their lives. They are making career changes, learning new sports, and accomplishing goals they never thought possible. It's especially apparent in women; as they learn to press barbells over their heads or successfully execute a pull up, their confidence levels soar.

Some of our clients have been able to go off type-2 diabetes medication because the doctor said they were no longer diabetic. Others have heard this unbelievable news from their doctor, "I see no signs of multiple sclerosis in your system anymore." Many times couples and entire families get involved in our program and find it is something that they can participate in and enjoy together. It gives them a common experience to talk about at night and look forward to the next day. In addition to reaping the benefits of healthier bodies, they are communicating more, and growing as couples and families. As crazy as it sounds, I have been thanked numerous times for saving marriages.

When we talk about a tribe-like culture, this is what it means: a place where people can experience amazing results in different aspects of their lives. When beginning the program, many will think, "I'm just coming to lose a few pounds." But, inevitably, they return to say, "Wow, this is so much more than I thought. I'm surprised I am enjoying it so much, and actually looking forward to each and every workout. This has truly changed my whole perspective."

There are barriers to entry—our system is expensive, exclusive, and hard—but those who chose to jump over these hurdles are incredible people. Our clients have made a commitment to be at our gym and they are "all in." They are comfortable with accountability. They know if they show up late, it's going to cost them. They know that if they don't do the form correctly, there are going to be ramifications. They have no issue with transparency, because there is no cheating. They are willing to work hard and continually improve, knowing that at the end of the workout their score is going to be posted on the leaderboard, the website, and the iPhone app for all to see. They can't hide behind a poor score or choose to participate only in things where they excel. Weaknesses get exposed, which creates instant humility; everyone quickly finds many things to work on.

Clients who can't handle competition or aren't willing to exert this type of effort either never get started or don't stick to the program long-term. This is perfectly fine with us—we know we're not for everyone, and realize our approach can be polarizing. The ones who stay often say, "You not only have the most amazing staff, but you also have the best clients. I love coming in just to hang out with everyone." It's a unique advantage to assemble such a wonderful group of clients. I have also had many tell me that the program has been self-funding for them; they have developed personal contacts with others in class and ended up doing business with them. Or, because they have been able to stop taking medication or lowered their life insurance premiums, they are saving money, even after paying the monthly membership dues.

We have been able to serve many different segments of the population. Although most of our classes are co-ed, we found that some women were too intimidated to train with men, so we offer women-only classes. Some of our most dramatic changes have come from women who didn't think they were competitive, and never imagined they would be pressing an Olympic barbell above their head, and then throwing it to the ground after a successful lift! I will never forget the middle-aged woman who came into my office trembling after her class. She had just led her teammates in a typical "break down" ritual where everyone puts their hands in the middle of the group and shouts, "3-2-1 TRIBE!" She told me that she had not played sports herself, yet had watched her kids break down a group after hundreds of sporting events. This was a thrilling milestone for her. A self-described non-competitive soccer mom, she never had the opportunity to compete, and was getting so much joy out of being part of a team that challenged each other and won together. The fact that she had lost 85 pounds along the way was a great side effect of training like an athlete and focusing on her performance.

The majority of our clients are 35 to 55 years old, which is surprising for many to hear. We actually have as many clients over 40 as we do under 40. Yet most people from the outside looking in think our clients must be under 30 and elite athletes, which has never been the case. Most of our clients have used a personal trainer or attended a boot camp in the past. They value the structure of accountability and coaching in their fitness routine, but were bored or weren't getting any results. We serve this segment of the popula-tion by offering an exciting, affordable, and effective program that reaps more than fitness. Because of this, we end up working with predominantly affluent middle- to upper-class clients who appreci-ate our services, values, and coaching. From our end, they are an absolute joy to work with.

Invariably, if one spouse joins our program, eventually the other spouse gets involved, too. Normally, they come in and say, "I'm so tired of hearing about this. I had to try it for myself." Now this dynamic is extending to their kids. When mom and dad are both talking about fitness and their results at the dinner table, the next question is, "Well, mom and dad, when can I start?"

Because of this, our clients who are parents literally begged us to start a children's program. Although we have never marketed Iron Tribe Kids externally, we have a thriving program at each location that works with youth from 6 to 13 years old. It is extremely gratifying to see the young ones grasp the fact that exercise can be fun, and it's something they can do their entire lives.

We also work with many business owners, CEOs, and key executives. They appreciate the team-building that happens at Iron Tribe, and often express a desire to transfer it to their work culture. I have to be careful here, not to go off chasing another opportunity. But there are a couple of things related to this that we've done successfully.

First, we've rolled out some corporate programs in which a business owner can sign up his or her employees and pay a discounted rate. At the end of the day, this is still private coaching, so it's not a cheap monthly membership, and not every business owner can afford it. Those who have used the program report results of great camaraderie and team building, decreased sick days, and increased productivity. Second, for some companies and their employees, we have offered special group workouts with specific team-building goals. This type of "corporate workout" is an untapped area that could be explored further, because our program encourages people to work together in a format other than the workplace, weaving together exercise, friendship, and fun.

We didn't invent this type of exercise program—it has been around for years. We didn't invent functional movements, group personal training, or the element of competition. What we *have* done is put it all together into a comprehensive program that is scalable, repeatable, and attractive to mainstream America. The end result is passionate clients who are achieving amazing results and becoming raving fans of the program. These fans and their referrals have ultimately allowed us to grow our corporate locations and to expand our franchise opportunity at a rapid pace.

To see examples of client testimonials, go to
www.irontribefranchise.com/book.

THE PALEO DIET

In their initial one-month-long beginners class called Iron Tribe 101, our clients are taught the Paleo diet. This way of eating is based on foods consumed in the Paleolithic, or hunter-gatherer, era. The dietary model is simply eating lean meats, vegetables, nuts, seeds, and fruits. Lean meats are protein sources that contain more grams of protein than fat. Examples include: turkey, chicken, fish, eggs, sirloin, steak filets, etc. Although nuts and seeds contain protein, we don't include them as sources of lean protein, because they have more grams of fat than lean meats. We encourage consumption of a broad selection of locally grown organic, non-starchy vegetables such as broccoli, squash, kale, and asparagus. Raw nuts and seeds are not only excellent sources of healthy dietary fats, but they also contain minerals and vitamins. Other beneficial foods we love are coconut oil and milk, olives and olive oil, almond butter, and ghee (clarified butter). Fruits are similar to vegetables, in the sense that we encourage consumption of a wide range of whole fruits. However, we discourage consumption of fruit juices, concentrates, and sauces, as they do not contain the fiber to help slow the absorption of the fruit's sugars into the blood stream.

The Paleo diet eliminates grains, dairy, legumes, sugars, processed foods, alcohols, and starchy vegetables. We understand that these foods are staples of our modern, agriculturally driven diet often referred to as the Standard American Diet, or SAD, for short. These food groups encourage inflammation, heart disease, obesity, hormonal disorders, and gastrointestinal disorders (to name a few). The Paleo diet is a paradigm shift from a carbohydrate-dependent diet to a fat and protein-dependent diet (the SAD recommends seven to 15 servings of carbohydrates per day).

Why do we recommend avoiding grains, dairy, legumes, sugars, processed foods, alcohols, and starchy vegetables? While there are numerous reasons for avoiding grains, the take-away is two-fold. One, they are extremely damaging to our guts, and two, they cause severe systemic inflammation. Dairy also causes systemic inflammation, as well as contains unnatural substances, such as antibiotics, puss, hormones (bovine growth hormone), and even blood. Sugar leads to obesity problems, causes insulin insensitivity, diabetes, and heart disease. We also encourage avoiding legumes, processed foods, starchy vegetables, and alcohols, as they negatively affect our health and performance.

Beverage consumption should be limited to water, organic coffee, and unsweetened teas. Almond and coconut milk can be used as a replacement in recipes. We encourage all our athletes to eliminate sodas, juices, non-organic coffee, and alcoholic beverages. Cutting out these beverages removes a large source of sugar and empty calories. We believe you should eat calories, not drink them.

With these simple dietary changes, we can remove the foods that negatively affect our health, while increasing our intake of foods full of vitamins, antioxidants, and minerals. When you combine this diet with our workout program, the results are incredibly effective!

For more information on creating Paleo meals, go to emeals.com.

WHY PALEO AT ITF?

We encourage the Paleo diet at ITF for many reasons, but mainly because it offers the BEST results for the MOST people! Members who implement this way of eating lose weight, look younger, feel better, and lower their chances of developing disease (cancer, diabetes, heart disease, Parkinson's and Alzheimer's, etc). It not only works for people in the weight-loss category, but it also helps improve athletic performance. In a nutshell, the Paleo diet helps people get to the best version of themselves. Does that mean this dietary model is perfect? No. Does that mean it is 100 percent right for everyone? No. If a better model evolves and is validated by scientific evidence, then we will migrate toward it and encourage it. However, the simple fact is that the Paleo diet continues to deliver the best results for the majority of our clients.

Another reason we feel secure in recommending the diet is because it has stood the test of time and significant scientific scrutiny. Anthropologists attest that our Paleolithic ancestors were remarkably healthy. They were tall, free of cavities and bone malformations (common with malnutrition), had a low infant mortality rate, and were free of degenerative diseases such as cancer, diabetes, and cardiovascular diseases. Furthermore, hunter-gatherers had powerful athletic builds, since they had to perform to survive.

The Paleo diet also improves digestion and related disorders. By removing grains and dairy, clients allow their guts to heal from issues of mal-absorption, celiac disease, Crohn's disease, and leaky gut. Once healed, other issues correct themselves, including infertility, type-1 diabetes, multiple sclerosis, rheumatoid arthritis, lupus, depression, and hypothyroidism (Rob Wolfe, *The Paleo Solution*, pg. 95). At ITF, specifically during our Transformation Challenges, we encourage our members to go strictly Paleo for 40 days. We have seen drastic improvements in our athlete's blood lipid panels and have had awesome testimonials of decreased cholesterol and decreased inflammation, as well as shocked physicians!

Furthermore, the Paleo diet encourages people toward their ideal body weight and composition. How much of a person's body is muscle and how much is fat is related to what a person eats. We believe that exercise is the spark and nutrition is the fuel for our athlete's metabolism and health. Our clients can exercise all they want, but until they master what they eat, they will never reach their health and fitness potential.

EVENTS

Once a client is committed to the workouts and nutritional aspect, they will naturally want to start competing at some of our events. We typically run two or three big charity events a year, but are careful not to create charity fatigue in our customers. We pick a couple of organizations that we feel we can impact significantly. On three out of four Saturdays each month, we hold some type of an event for our customers. It may be a workshop on goal setting or nutrition, or a skills workshop where clients concentrate on jumping rope, climbing a rope, or a move they're not comfortable with, such as a clean and jerk. Or, all of the tribes might come together to participate in a challenge, complete with judges.

Events take competition in the daily workout to a higher level, as members compete with the other members from different locations. What happens at the individual store level is magnified during these Saturday gatherings—clients connect with each other, learn tools and techniques, and advance their fitness. On these days, many have run into a co-worker who attends a class at a different time than they do, not realizing they were both going to the same location. When all of the stores come together, typically someone from one part of the city sees someone from another area and says, "I didn't know you were going to Iron Tribe." Each connection builds community, reinforces feelings of belonging to the tribe, and fosters mutual encouragement.

At the same time, the venues give members an outlet for competing. Frankly, the degree to which our athletes have embraced this aspect and continue to ask for more ways to compete has surprised me. As they are competing every day in the workouts, a desire is created to test how they stack up against other people. It is clear they enjoy the challenge, and we are only limited by our own creativity in providing it for them. To answer this need, we have created individual, team, partner, and 5K competitions in which members do workouts along the 5K route. In our March Madness event, a bracket is used similar to the one in college basketball. Members compete against each other, and winners advance through the bracket until, ultimately, a final winner remains. In the Transformation Challenge held twice a year, clients train for 40 days, during which they compare results on weight loss, blood panel results, reduction in cholesterol, and reduction in inflammation. We give away more than $10,000 in prizes after each Transformation Challenge. All of this creates vitality and excitement, and builds an environment that becomes more than a gym experience. It's a lifestyle, one that is effective in changing people's lives.

THE RIGHT STAFF

Many of our best staff members initially start as clients. One of the great benefits of this business model is the ability to watch people over an extended period of time, seeing them perform continually in different kinds of circumstances. I am able to discern if they possess characteristics I look for in an employee: Do they show up consistently? Are they on time? Do they do everything that's required? Do they cheat or are they honest? Are they open to coaching? Do they come to events? Do they help out even when they're not being paid? It's like a secret on-the-job interview. By the time I'm ready to make an offer to someone, I already know much about him or her, because I've observed their character and responses to challenge, hard work, and training. It eliminates the guesswork in hiring.

I often hear other business owners talking about the difficulty in their company's interview process. They create hypothetical circumstances for potential employees, in an attempt to determine their true character. Whether it's shadowing a current employee for a day, taking a shift on his or her own, or meeting with other employees, the processes tend to be hit or miss. The statistics on the ones they hire and those that stick around are not always great.

Eventually, I realized I have that process "baked into the model." That's the reason we've had such good internal hires. Jim, who's now the COO, started as a client. Karen Florence, our operation implementer, was first a client, then a manager at one of our stores, and now works in the corporate office. Richard Martens, who started as a part-time coach, ultimately became our first franchisee. We're able to hire and develop the cream of the crop!

We start with a pool of incredible athletes who work out together, share our core values, and demonstrate transparency and accountability. My coaches and I keep an eye on those who have consistent performance and who may be a good fit within our culture. I have detailed systems in the selection of potential candidates, the interview process itself, and the on- and off-the-floor training for the first 90 days.

I told the story earlier about how Jim approached me about a job six months after joining Iron Tribe. I knew he had his own business, and I could see he was technologically savvy. He'd created a website that helped high school athletes get recruited and land scholarships, and he was selling it to high school associations all over the Southeast. He fell in love with what we were doing, and when he approached me about joining the team, I was as eager as he was to make that happen.

Jim sold his business and quickly moved from being a coach to running the second store. Now as a partner, Jim has raised the level of technological sophistication, systemization, and experience in the entire company. His contribution goes way beyond technology, since he oversees and builds the operating systems for Iron Tribe as a whole. We would not be where we are today without him.

The Right Team

Luan Nguyen, our director or training, worked with me in some capacity for more than 10 years. I knew from the beginning that I had to have an expert focused on the product each and every day. Luan has filled that key position and allowed us to maintain product excellence, while growing the business systems and tools at the same time. As head of our product development team, Luan not only creates the workouts performed each day, but is also responsible for the coaches' development, standardizing the program through videos on our internal website, and daily interactions with our corporate staff and franchisees. Luan ran his own personal training studio for eight years, and managed several of our ITF locations. His operations experience has been invaluable.

Karen Florence was one of those clients who consistently showed up, helped, and always had a smile on her face. She started in an administration position in 2010, but quickly moved to managing our number-one store in 2011. Then in 2012, she was the third employee on the franchise side in an operations-implementer role. Before she joined our team, she provided group benefits for businesses, a job she wasn't passionate about. When she first came to us as a client, she was 40 pounds overweight and was motivated to do something about it. Early on, she attended one of my goal-setting workshops that she doesn't mind telling people literally changed her life. Unknown to us, one of the goals she wrote down after the workshop was to work at Iron Tribe. We noticed her great work ethic and consistently positive attitude, and realized she could be a potential fit for the organization. When we gave her an opportunity with us, she grabbed it with both hands. What a great story to watch unfold!

Richard Martens' story, which I also told earlier, says a lot about the fitness industry as a whole. There are not many career opportunities for those who want to coach or own their own fitness business.

They either work for a big gym, train clients, and pay a percentage of revenue to the gym, or they train on their own and build up a client base, but are limited by the number of hours in a day and the amount they can charge. As with most trainers, their passion is training. They have a hard time making a living and end up supplementing their income by becoming real estate agents or bartenders. I see many of these trainers who, if they thought they could truly make a career out of their passion, would jump at the opportunity. That's how Richard responded. His job selling commercial real estate wasn't his passion, either—it was just paying the bills. When he started to look at an opportunity with us as we opened our second store, he saw an organization where he could put his passion to work, and build a career at the same time. He started as a part-time employee, but eventually quit selling commercial real estate when we moved him to head coach. He later managed our second store and became our first franchisee.

Chelsey McIntyre is another success story. She worked for us for 18 months, and is now moving back to Atlanta to open three locations with her husband and two other clients. One of my original staff members, Tra Griffin, started as a coach. As a Marine and personal trainer, he had a lot of fitness knowledge, but no direction in his career. He was about to leave the fitness industry when I hired him. He has moved from part-time coach to managing the largest location, and is now the Birmingham area director responsible for overseeing and managing our six stores. Because he is the right man for the job, and because we have built a proven and clear career path, we are able to provide him with a long-term plan. He is performing at a very high level, which is profitable for both of us.

These are the stories of successful hires I want to continue throughout our organization. I want to give the right team players an opportunity to build a career by working in the stores in Birmingham or in one of our franchised locations. There are many opportunities to coach clients, manage stores, work at the corporate office, or support franchised locations as they open. This may lead to an opportunity to quickly learn the system, partner with an investor, and open his or her own franchise location. That's a key focus for us—to grow people and provide careers. Our desire to turn coaches into businessmen and women has been realized by successfully hiring internally and teaching the business skills necessary to work for us.

Because we have experienced such tremendous growth through franchising, the need for highly qualified and trained manager operators has skyrocketed. The majority of our owners are investors who are passionate about the brand, yet are looking to us to help them find and develop outstanding operators. These operators must execute the model, align with the core values, match the personality profiles specified for the position, and have a passion for helping people change their lives through fitness. We started working with a company called FireSeeds (**www.fireseeds.com**), which specializes in recruiting and hiring the right people. We initially tested their services at our corporate stores and, when we saw the depth and quality of applicants they were bringing us, quickly rolled them out to all of our franchisees. Together with FireSeeds, we have developed an in-depth, comprehensive program that takes months for an applicant to get through. However, the ones that finally make it to a sit-down interview, along with an "on the floor coaching" with my team, are the cream of the crop. Because this process has proven successful in both corporate and franchise stores, we are using the same process in hiring coaches, as well.

With the success of turning coaches into leaders, we replicated this model for our franchisees. They can now use our Manager

Practicum Program (MPP) and Coaches Practicum Program (CPP) to bring their coaches and managers/operators into our corporate stores. Once a candidate finally makes it all the way through our recruiting and hiring process with FireSeeds, they spend six weeks in our system learning everything they need to know in order to open and operate their own location. This provides the opportunity to receive on-the-job training by coaching classes, shadowing our managers, role-playing in different types of client interactions, sitting in on the sales process, and going through data entry in the software program. They practice executing the model, and dramatically accelerate their learning curve. By the time they open their location, they hit the ground running, because they know exactly what to do. More importantly, they have the Iron Tribe DNA infused into them. They leave knowing what the culture of their gym should look like through spending time in our six gyms and learning from our all-star coaching and management staff!

CHAPTER 7

THE TECHNOLOGY ACCELERATOR

We knew we couldn't depend on "superstars" to replicate the Iron Tribe system—it needed to be simple enough for anyone to reproduce. Even though we weren't marketing to "average" operators—we were doing everything in our power to recruit and train superstars—we knew the system had to work for everyone. What we needed was a central repository where all the information we had developed, tested, and built over the last three years could be accessed and implemented.

To continue executing the model at a high level and keeping it consistent as we opened more of our own stores, as well as franchised locations, we needed a robust customer relations management (CRM) system. This system would pull everything together, giving managers daily, weekly, and monthly checklists with detailed action steps. We investigated multiple options, and eventually selected Infusionsoft as our CRM. Although Infusionsoft's program immediately gave us additional capacity, we spent hundreds of hours building it to our unique specifications, including models for messages, emails, and sequences. This information was formatted in a template, which ensured that all locations communicated with every prospect and client in exactly the same way. After integrating this software, we experienced even more impressive growth. We immediately began to see an increase in leads, which converted to customers, and resulted in a higher closing rate. Customers stayed longer and referred others more frequently. Thinking through each customer interaction and every responsibility of coaches and managers provided a method for consistent, repeatable success. Nothing was left to chance, and everything was automated. This reduced human error and created a uniform experience for our members and franchisees.

LEVERAGING TECHNOLOGY TO
REPLICATE THE MODEL

To ensure the system was even more effective, we designed a separate website with an application that communicated directly to Infusion-soft. When franchisees signed on with us, they got immediate access to this network of information. They received a step-by-step plan of implementation, with specific documents to read and study based on their current level in the development process of their own franchise. Whether they were in site selection, lease negotiation, construction management, or the grand opening phase, everything was chrono-logically laid out for them. They watched online web modules and were quizzed afterwards. All of this prepared them for the next stage of development, whch eventually culminated with the day-to-day operation of their business.

The system tracked everything the franchisee and manager needed to do at the store level, but it also guided them every step of the way to make sure their store opened on schedule and on budget.

We used our experience of building six stores and created processes, systems, and videos on every aspect of development. This allowed us to create an all-encompassing platform that shortened the learning curve and maximized profitability of the stores.

Because we continued to open and operate our own stores, we knew exactly *what* managers and franchisees should be doing, and *when* it should be done. We documented every aspect required for growth: checklists, videos, and supplemental reading resources. This information was posted on the online membership site, and became a road map for managers and franchisees. The site enabled them to be laser-focused on delivering an excellent experience to customers, and reaching the break-even point and profitability level as quickly as possible. Whether they needed to know how to determine the best site, plan for the construction phase, set up a gym for the daily workout, or run a weekend event, there was a video, PDF document, webinar, screencast, or checklist available.

We also developed operations manuals, but knew it would be easier (and more powerful) for franchisee owners to access technology. Being able to search for videos by keywords and tags reduced search time, so a manager wouldn't have to look through a big three-ring binder, trying to find an answer to his or her question. A franchisee could quickly pull up their proprietary membership website, search by keyword or topic, and find exactly what they're looking for. Although this was a huge project, the impact has been immense. The franchisees who are implementing the website are realizing tremendous value from it by shortening their learning curve and giving them more time to focus on the acquisition and retention of new members.

KEY PERFORMANCE INDICATORS

I'm a believer in running your business by the numbers, and the only way to accomplish that is by knowing what your numbers are. We've tracked our numbers from the beginning. At first, this involved multiple Excel spreadsheets and manual systems. Now the information is tracked and managed automatically through our proprietary software system "The Bay Door." We use every tool available to follow metrics that have a bearing on the performance or success of the clients and business. We tracked the criteria, pinpointed where we were in the process, and figured out how to constantly improve and replicate the metrics.

In the end, the Key Performance Indicator (*KPI*) system was able to measure approximately 25 key performance indicators. Tracked automatically through our system, they enable us to evaluate our corporate stores and those of our franchisees to make sure they were executing the model correctly. We track phone calls from potential customers, the percentage of calls that turn into an appointment, the percentage of appointments that turn into sales, the percentage of renewals resulting from the sale, the percentage of customers who use our food program, and the revenue or expenses for the month. These key performance indicators helped us objectively evaluate a particular store or manager so we can see whether they are underperforming or exceeding the norms across our stores. Once we knew this vital information, we were able to provide the specific tools and systems needed to improve their numbers and get them back on track.

CHAPTER 8

MARKETING TO SUCCESS

A t Iron Tribe, we're marketers and we're proud of it. We think marketing provides the best way to influence our prospects and customers. If we can't get them in, we can't change their lives. When a customer sits across the desk from us in a consult, we know the greatest thing we can do is give them knowledge about the Iron Tribe program. We're so confident in our program we believe anyone who hears about it will want to get involved immediately!

We don't believe marketing is separate from fitness. We think it is all one and the same, and there is no dichotomy between the two. We spend considerable resources hiring consultants who have specialties in everything from list brokering to copywriting to design. Together, we develop campaigns that incorporate a direct response element. We can track the amount of interest each campaign generates, trace the interest back to the cost, and evaluate return on the investment. We demand to know the type of return each campaign generates, and because we know the average client value, we calculate the amount we're willing to spend to generate a new client. This allows us to not only build campaigns that are self-funding and generate substantial returns, but also to constantly test and build new campaigns.

For instance, during the writing of this book, I've been working on a campaign for prospects who have not made a buying decision. They know about us, they've raised their hands to indicate their interest, and have even given us their contact information. But for some reason, they didn't schedule a consultation or join our program. How do we reach these potential customers and provide another opportunity to make a life-changing buying decision? My new campaign will target this special group; it will be tested, refined, and proven effective in our six stores before becoming part of the model.

When you look at the reasons people fail when entering this business (and so many do), it is usually because they're involved in the *details* of the business—running the day-to-day program, and concentrating on the coaching aspect. They think the *marketing* and sales component is the antithesis of what they love to do. They often believe, "If you build it, they will come." So they do not market at all, and completely rely on word-of-mouth advertising and referrals. Although referrals are tremendously important, it is a drastic mistake to rely only on them to build business.

We still get great word-of-mouth recommendations and referrals, but we don't count on them alone to build our businesses. We build detailed marketing plans. We pay for consultants to help us tweak and maximize our campaigns. In this way, we become even more referable. When a client says something about Iron Tribe, undoubtedly the prospects have seen the ads, the billboards, and the buildings. Their friend's words connect with what they've already seen, and they respond, "Oh yeah, I've heard of them." When they come in to try us out, we give them the same consistent experience that their referring friend has had. Clients can refer friends with confidence—they know we are going to deliver the same life-changing program they are already enjoying.

That's one of the reasons for our success. We help our franchisees implement this process by providing a specific plan for the first 150 days. We instruct them: "Send this piece of direct mail out in January. Send this one in February. Put this ad in the paper, and run this referral contest coupled with an event and a Transformation Challenge." They are able to operate from a clear-cut plan, which has been executed in our corporate stores. It is their road map to proven results.

Direct Response Marketing Program

Some of Our Many Marketing Examples

FOLLOW THE LEADS

Leads come from many different avenues. We know we must be diversified in the use of media to truly create ubiquity. We constantly tell our franchisees—we can't show you one way to get 100 clients, but we can show you 100 ways to get one client! We are prolific on social media, constantly run events, advertise on billboards, send direct mail, and place ads in magazines and newspapers, and we have a whole system designed to motivate people to make one of two responses.

The number-one response we want potential clients to make: call or visit one of our facilities. Once they get in the door, they can go on a tour, sit down with one of our managers, and go through a diagnostic consultation process. This gives us the chance to find out more about the prospect's needs, background, and history. We need to understand his or her goals in order to make recommendations that are a good fit for them.

For those who don't have the confidence to call or come in, we offer a second response: simply raise their hand and say they have an interest. We have multiple low-threat and low-barrier ways for them to do this. They can either put themselves on our e-mail campaign or give us their contact information. This enables us to send information on the program, share testimonials, and answer every question they might have. We want to provide anything they need to know in order to make a positive buying decision. We'll also mail a free 30-page report, which is jam-packed with details of the program's benefits. They are able to read for themselves the testimonials and success stories, which show that anyone can workout at Iron Tribe and receive amazing results.

Through the process of educating people via the web, videos, and direct mail, prospects already understand who we are by the time they come in for a consultation. We've been able to build rapport, and they've become comfortable with us. At that point, we are able to have effective conversations about their needs and desires. Ultimately, this process leads them to become a client, and we are able to make a sale. In fact, more than 94 percent of the prospects who have booked a consultation with our managers in Birmingham have become clients!

For direct mail, we typically buy a customer list based on different factors, such as drive time to the location, household income, gender, and age. The list can be broken down into fitness preferences, selecting only those who are members of a gym or subscribers to a fitness magazine. Specifics about potential clients can be entered, resulting in a perfect message crafted for that prospect that will hopefully lead them to make one of the two responses above.

At the store level, we can know how many leads were generated, what percentage of those leads should be converted to consultations, and what percentage of the consultations should be converted to sales. Once the sale is made, we can follow the customers by documenting how often they renew, the rate of renewal, and any other desired statistic that helps determine whether a store is executing the model correctly.

This is crucial information in a marketing effort, and where so many business owners miss the connection. The average lifetime client value is established through these markers: the average conversion time for first-time purchases, how many times the average client renews, how much they spend on profit centers, and how many referrals they give.

Understanding the value of each customer and how much worth an individual client brings to the table is essential. It allows the manager or franchisee to calculate, "This is the amount I'm willing to spend to get a new customer. I understand every client is worth X, so it makes sense to spend Y." Not following leads or realizing the value of each potential client are huge missing steps in many businesses. Owners seem to have the attitude, "What's the least amount I can spend to get a customer?" instead of taking into account what that customer is actually worth over their lifetime of membership.

CLOSING THE SALE

Selling from a place of abundance versus scarcity is the hallmark of our brand message. The Tribe mentality, our culture, and our message says, "We know we're not for everybody and we realize if you don't want to work hard, if you can't handle transparency, if you're not competitive ... well, our program may not be a good fit." However, we've found that many clients say they aren't competitive at the beginning of the program, yet turn out to be some of our most competitive members.

If a client is willing to change his or her life by investing in a program and being held accountable, then our program can be a great fit. We're not looking for thousands of people—only 300—and when that cap is reached, we're not going to add additional memberships. This allows us to cater the experience to the clients we have.

We know our clients by their first names. We know when they don't show up, or when they are off for a week. We're aware of an injury they are dealing with, and we modify the workout accordingly. The tailor-made environment allows us to deliver a niche experience, which is not possible to achieve at the huge gyms.

I don't care how nice the "big box" gyms are or how well staffed they are. Their staff members often don't know the customers' names. The clients are lost in the shuffle; if they don't show up, no one knows. The clients don't know anyone else working out there, so there's no sense of community.

Iron Tribe's sales mentality is different from the average big-gym model. We try to determine if we have a mutual fit with a customer and if this is truly a long sustainable program that they can excel at. Again, we are creating much more than just a gym. We become family. One of our taglines states, *"We are more than a gym, we are a tribe of athletes."*

We realize there are 300 people in the community who *will* fit our program—we just have to find the right ones. We don't have to sell to "anyone and everyone." Those who join our team feel a sense of exclusivity in knowing they are part of a unique experience. There is a bit of pride in being associated with Iron Tribe and becoming one of our athletes.

Many people admire our growth, marketing strategies and lead-generated sales, and are impressed by the number of clients we sign up in a month. We are proud of these accomplishments and don't shy away from the fact that we are marketers. We don't hide from this essential ingredient to success; instead, we embrace it as a central part of our business. Probably the one aspect I take the most pride in is our attrition numbers. If we're great at marketing, have a compelling story, and get a bunch of people through the door—it doesn't mean anything if they're not getting results and are going out the back door faster than they're coming in. When that happens, typical comments are: "It wasn't worth it," "It's OK," "It's just all hype," or "It didn't work for me." This kind of negative press will negate any marketing message, and create a cycle of failure that is hard to overcome. We have been so focused on keeping the retention numbers high that we have been able to achieve less than 3 percent monthly attrition rate across our six stores in the Birmingham market!

ON THE WEB

The Web has become an increasingly important part of our business model. We have spent considerable time creating a great website and making sure it is customer friendly. Members can communicate with each other through the site, almost in a Facebook-type manner. They can record scores, keep a profile, and view comments from other members of the Iron Tribe community.

I think the reason we won Ultimate Marketers of the Year was because of how we leveraged technology for our bricks and mortar locations to expand rapidly. Our success was related to the number of leads we generated and captured, expanded into consults, and inevitably converted into customers. Our Internet strategy was an integral part of the whole process.

The statistics are compelling. In 2010 when we first opened, the majority of our prospects were responding to us using the "A" or first-option offer by either calling us or walking in. That meant they didn't start the education process until they talked with a person. As we put our CRM and Internet strategies into place, we generated the "B" or second option, which mailed or delivered the information digitally. This option was the perfect answer for those who are hesitant, intimidated, undecided, or who desire more information without having to talk to someone. During the first month we implemented this system, it automatically delivered 18 emails that educated people on the program through video, text, and testimonials.

In 2010, all of our customers were walking in or inquiring by phone. In 2011, with the new processes in place, half of our customers were coming from phone calls and walk-ins, and half were coming through the Internet. In 2012, and now well into 2013, the majority of prospects came through the Internet already educated about Iron Tribe.

Because these potential customers can read the information on our websites and ahead of time, they are more likely to quickly sign up when they come in. They're pre-sold. They feel like they already have a relationship with us, understand the program, and are ready to do business with us. Marketing online does the heavy lifting as far as the sales process goes. My managers sometimes tell me, "It's not sales anymore. I'm now taking an order and giving a prescription. They come in already sold, knowing they want to do it. I simply help them pick the right program and get them signed up." Creating ways for potential customers to get educated without having to come in has been invaluable, because it saves my staff's time, increases the sales percentage, and gives the client the information they need to know on their terms without having to be sold.

We have also used other web initiatives, such as SEO (search engine optimization), SEM (search engine marketing), and keyword searches, to generate response and supplement our offline marketing. During this process of incorporating additional marketing strategies, we learned that, not only do we need SEO and SEM, but we also need to be managing our online brand reputation. With Google emphasizing its "Places" page, it was possible to have negative reviews posted without our knowledge. We needed to have a watchdog on the web, with systems specifically focused on managing our online reputation.

Often times, people use the maps feature on their iPhone to call an Iron Tribe gym. When they type in our name, the app brings up Google Places, along with associated reviews of the business. As potential customers increasingly rely on these reviews to make a purchase, a bad online reputation might mean they won't come to our gym. By managing our Google Places accounts, proactively rewarding good reviews, and creating an entire system that insures our online reputation matches our offline reputation, our sales are that much easier to generate. Continued good reviews build trust—not only with prospects, but also with current clients.

When we receive negative feedback—and, invariably, a business will—we have a system in place to address it. When a negative tweet or comment shows up on a Facebook page, we respond to it immediately. In this way, everyone who follows Iron Tribe in the social media world and is in our sphere of influence sees that, yes, we make mistakes, but we're going to do the right thing to correct them.

We also have a plan for dealing with competitors who lurk about on the sites and post comments regarding how expensive we are, stating their services are cheaper. This ugly part of a competitive business is to be expected and, when it comes, has to be managed. Most potential customers can see through the noise and under-stand when a competitor or a hater makes a negative comment. We respond appropriately, and the customer sees us taking the high road. In today's marketplace, it is unrealistic to expect to be successful in business without generating negativity from others. But addressing each negative person or comment with integrity and allowing the whole world to listen to our response can counter this.

Here's an example: a guy recently sent us a tweet that said, "Old-fashioned spam is still spam. Quit sending me your direct mail pieces." Instead of taking offense at his comment, we addressed it by sending a simple tweet that said, "Sorry. We'll immediately remove you from our list." Because he was on our mailing list and we had his full contact info, we also sent him a $10 gift card to a local restau-

rant. When he received the handwritten card containing the gift certificate, he tweeted that we were amazing people and he was thankful
for the gesture. This led others to tweet us, asking to be spammed
so they could get a gift card! We turned a negative situation into a
positive one and successfully managed our online reputation. We're
not always going to make everybody happy, but ... we give it our best
effort. Ultimately, the success of a positive customer online experience depends on establishing a great website, marketing the website,
and actively managing the brand's reputation.

SOCIAL MEDIA

Dan Kennedy Has Been a Great Mentor

Jim and I are co-authoring a book to be released next year with
marketing legend Dan Kennedy, *No BS Brand Building through
Direct Response Marketing*. In this book, we share secrets of using
direct response marketing to build a brand. The basic principle is
built around expecting a quantifiable return on every dollar spent
on direct-response advertising. If we spend $2,000 to send 2,000

postcards and, as a result, sign up three customers who generate $6,000 on the initial purchase, then we have realized a 300 percent return on investment (ROI). Three hundred percent is our goal for every campaign. Of course, the real value is to know the customer's lifetime value, as mentioned previously. That ultimate return is much greater than 300 percent from the initial purchase because of the longevity of the relationship with our customers.

In the case of Twitter, Facebook, LinkedIn, and other social media, we focus more on return of engagement rather than return on investment. We don't use those media to sell memberships. For example, we would never make a comment on our Facebook page such as, "Come in today and receive a $99 membership."

The people we address on social media are our *customers*. We use it to create engagement and community. We share photos taken in class, talk about the great job they are doing, post a link to a helpful blog, or suggest a recipe they might enjoy. We try to create conversation, which expands the brand through engaging our clients. Probably the biggest reason companies fail using social media is because they treat it like any other medium by pushing a company's message, sales pitch, or brand. We have found that social media is not a place to push but an opportunity to listen, engage, and ask questions like, "What was your favorite part about the workout today?" Pushing can actually lead to fewer results and less conversation.

When customers engage in an online conversation with us, the tribe experience is expanded beyond the 45-minute workout that day. As we interact during the through conversation and photo tags, we show up in customers' news feeds seen by their friends. We've definitely experienced value return from social media; we just don't push or generate that return. Focusing on using social media to build relationships with current customers yields the best results, and allows new business to be generated organically.

THE BRANDING

When developing Iron Tribe initially, I knew brand development was crucial. Therefore, I spent a tremendous amount of time, energy, and money creating a brand around the tribe concept. I was meticulous about every aspect working together and playing off the other in order to create an engaging and cohesive brand image. The logo was taken from a digital clock, because everything we do in the workout is timed. The brand colors, the mark, tag lines, and facility build outs are coordinated—every detail is considered, even down to the color of the pull-up bars! I want our brand to stand out and for a customer to recognize they are walking into an Iron Tribe gym, whether it's in Birmingham or Denver.

We are careful to design cool-looking apparel that would appeal to everyone. We regularly give bumper stickers, bracelets, and signature clothing to our customers so they can spread our message around town. We create new shirts for every event, enabling our customers to sport fresh Iron Tribe gear every few months. When people all over town are wearing shirts and bracelets and have stickers on their cars, others notice and say, "What *is* this Iron Tribe thing?" And because our clients are so passionate about their experience, they don't mind telling others what it is all about! These small—and sometimes subtle—things create a brand and a movement that sets you apart from your competitors. We have been voted best gym in Birmingham every year since we opened, and I think one of the reasons is that we're ubiquitous and we have a strong memorable brand.

Every franchisee has a brand standards manual that specifies the look of an Iron Tribe gym and stipulates how they should use the brand and the mark in advertising. This develops brand consistency throughout our locations. We have also chosen to be involved in the site selection, lease negotiation, and construction management process, which ensures an Iron Tribe in Brentwood looks just like an Iron Tribe in Birmingham. While traveling in Tennessee, Birmingham customers have dropped in and worked out with Richard in Brentwood. They inevitably come back and tell me, "Man, it felt like home! It was just like working out here." That's all part of the brand experience. No matter where they travel in the country, the Iron Tribe experience is the same.

BECOME THE EXPERT

We first ask our managers, as well as our franchisees, to be ambassadors for the brand. This includes everything from "guerrilla marketing" to knocking on doors. It means getting to know neighboring businesses by going to chamber meetings and seeking speaking opportunities. These activities are next to impossible to engage in when managers are so busy inside the business they can't get outside its four walls. Our carefully developed systems free them up to focus on these important aspects.

Second, it is critical that they become the fitness expert in their community. We tell them to be on the lookout for speaking opportunities; when they are the speaker, they are automatically the experts. Writing press releases, newsletters, free reports, posts for customer-relevant blogs, and even books are incredible expert positioning tools and resources for clients. And well-written tools can set them apart from every other fitness business in their city. Focusing on building the tools and resources that allow clients and potential customers to view the Iron Tribe team as the go-to experts for fitness and health cannot be emphasized enough.

Once the customer becomes a client, everything possible is done to make sure he or she has a great experience and reports it to their friends. This creates buzz and the "stickiness factor" mentioned earlier. People will want to be involved, to be part of the tribe, and to feel a part of something bigger than just working out. It all goes back to marketing, advertising, and branding. This means we don't stop selling once a customer joins! We are constantly selling exclusivity, a sense of belonging, and our expert status in order to solve fitness needs and goals. This will give both current and potential customers complete confidence in joining, renewing, and referring us to others as the experts they trust with every area regarding their health and fitness.

Our clients help us become the experts through their feedback. We make it a priority to listen to what they have to say by sending out two surveys a year. They are asked detailed questions about their likes and dislikes, the services they wish we offered, or the elements they wish we didn't offer. We love to ask questions like, "What do you hope we never stop doing? What do you wish we would absolutely stop doing? Are there additional class times you'd like to see?" We let them tell us every single thing they desire in the model so we can create it to their satisfaction. Any time our staff members are in a one-on-one conversation with a customer, they are trained to ask at some point, "What could we be doing better?"

No doubt about it—our most valuable information comes straight from our clients. Our chef-prepared meal program, snack line, and supplement line all came from listening to their feedback.

For instance, when they wanted to know our recommendations regarding fish oil, multivitamins, or post-workout recovery shakes, we not only provided products, but also created workshops and events to provide information and meet their needs.

Because we found the feedback so insightful, we established a client committee of handpicked customers across our six stores. The ones chosen were members who had been with us from the beginning, as well as those who had recently signed up. When we bring them together for honest conversation, we ask hard questions to get the honest truth straight from the ones who are experiencing our services. They tell it like it is! When we're doing right, they compliment us, but they also have the freedom to let us know when we are dropping the ball.

Again, it allows us to go back to the drawing board. We are spurred on to ask, "How can we create a better user experience in the gym or online site?" At one of our last meetings, some clients voiced frustration over how cumbersome it was to schedule classes online. Thankfully, that was due to a limitation of the third-party software we used. The clients didn't know we were just about to release our own proprietary software system, The Bay Door, which completely eliminated the scheduling challenges.

Customers not only become our teachers, but also help us put our resources in the right places. As a result, we better serve our clients and, in the process, become the experts they continue to rely on.

ATTRITION

We enjoy high retention and low attrition rates in every one of our Iron Tribe gyms. I really believe that is a natural overflow of listening to the consumer and focusing on their experience. Our goal is no more than 3 percent attrition a month, and we've been able to maintain that number across the six stores. We've become good at weeding out people who don't fit the program. The indicators are consistent: they don't want to work hard, don't "get" what we do, or they want to perform a body-part specific workout system

Of course, we lose some people because they move to another city, which is out of our control. Others occasionally get injured because they are training like an athlete and, as in all sports, injuries occur. But we do everything in our power to limit injuries. Other clients simply can't afford a membership long term. And, some people who end up leaving tell us, "This is too intense and I can't work out this hard." We're okay with that, because having an unmotivated client will actually hurt the dynamic of the group. We focus on creating the best environment for our members, and that is determined, in large part, by the dynamics of their group. If everyone is motivated, excited about the program, and getting results, then it makes our 3 percent attrition goal extremely achievable!

THE TRIBE TOUCH

The general fitness model is broken. So many people join a gym but, for one reason or another, never end up going. From my perspective, it's getting harder and harder for the big gyms to attract clients, because customers are looking for more than a gym experience. With that in mind, we try to ensure that our clients receive a personal touch each day. They are called by their first names when they come into the facility. They are cheered during workouts or challenged to press harder. We look them in the eyes when they speak. And, every month they receive what we call a "Tribe Touch."

The Tribe Touch happens as a staff member, whether a coach or manager, reaches out personally to a client. They can do this by making a phone call, writing a note, or posting a message on Facebook or Twitter. The only requirement is that the message be personalized and not generic. In these Tribe Touches, our staff refers to the client's goals, their good attitude in class, or their great work ethic on a particular WOD (workout of the day).

Our excellent automated system and advanced technology ensures the program is consistent. If someone is overlooked for a Tribe Touch, they are flagged at the end of the month. In this way, we know every active member received a personal touch that month. The clients know their goals are important to us, and that they are not "just a number." Continued personal interaction plays heavily into the retention process. We want people to come. We're worried when people don't show up, because if they don't come, they don't hit their goals. If they don't reach their goals, they don't renew. If they don't renew, they don't refer. It's a vicious cycle.

We don't want to be like the normal fitness model, where excess clients are signed up and then management hopes they don't show up. We want to sign a few up and make sure each one gets everything they desire out of the program.

Some of our very first clients are still coming in and working out more than three years later. Every single person who began in my garage experiment is still involved. Two of them have gone on to purchase multiple franchises, and neither one had a background in fitness! The Iron Tribe experience changed their lives. They were so impacted by the brand they decided to combine their knowledge of business with their passion for fitness and partner with us to grow the concept in new territories. The Iron Tribe touch made all the difference.

THE READING LIST

People know that I am a voracious reader and have a large personal library. I mentioned earlier how some of our motivated staff and members asked me to recommend reading material. Not only have I made my personal library available, but we have also put a page on our web site with recommended reading lists, complete with quizzes for my staff to take to make sure they're retaining the knowledge.

I've already mentioned it several times, so it is probably no surprise that one of my all-time favorite business books is *The E-Myth*, by Michael Gerber. Reading this book in 2001 was an eye opener for me as I performed day-to-day on the floor. It helped me build a business that didn't depend on me doing all the work. It helped me develop systems and processes for every single aspect of the business, which ensured uniformity and enabled it to be repro-duced in hundreds of stores. His words still challenge me to create something bigger and better, and to continue to offer opportunity to others. I try to read the book once a year and invariably learn something new, as each year I am in a different phase of my business development.

I'm also a big fan of *Good to Great*, by Jim Collins. I have found all of his books applicable and useful in my business. I especially love the lesson from *Good to Great* about getting the "right team on the bus" and focusing on your "hedgehog concept," or the thing you can be best at in the world. It has been surprising to see that, as Iron Tribe has grown, the problem is not *lack* of opportunity but *too much* opportunity! I tend to see opportunity everywhere, but have to be disciplined in remembering our "hedgehog" and pursue it with all our energy. It's easy to get distracted.

I love the Zappos story in *Delivering Happiness*, and the Starbucks story in *Pour Your Heart Into It*. I really connect with stories of others in start-up businesses who are passionate about their brand and customer service. Because of this passion, they develop a business that becomes a household name. We often share ideas from these types of books with our staff, using them to motivate all of us. By learning from others' examples, we create value and meaning for our athletes.

At first, the Starbucks experience described in *Pour Your Heart Into It* was all about the coffee. But in Howard Schultz's latest book, *Onward*, he shares how the company got away from this main focus and started emphasizing growth more than a deep and abiding love for coffee. He had to step back in as CEO and re-infuse the organization with a love for the product, which ultimately led to their turnaround. I identify strongly with stories like this, as they motivate me to stay true to our mission. We need to stay true to who we are as a company, and continue to create results at the individual athlete level.

I'm also a fan of the book *Steve Jobs* by Walter Isaacson, although I don't want to emulate his management practices or his quirky behaviors. I do love his absolute passion for design and excellence, and how it drove everything he did. Even when it didn't make sense to others, and the engineers were pulling their hair out, he was focused on the user experience and design that ultimately made Apple what it is today.

Equally as impressive to me is Arnold Schwarzenegger's book, *Total Recall*. Although many people are quick to dismiss him because of his recent marital troubles, I have always found Arnold to be an amazing leader and communicator. When you read the book, you cannot help but be awed by the life of this European immigrant, the people he calls friends, and what he has accomplished. I defy you to flip through his book, look at the pictures, and not be blown away by what this man has accomplished. He has always been one of my greatest heroes, and I hope to meet him one day!

To see more of my top book selections, visit
www.irontribefranchise.com/book.

THE TRUTH ABOUT THE FITNESS BUSINESS

Just like my experience, most people who enter the fitness business are trainers who have a passion for fitness, but who don't know anything about business. They end up being frustrated while working for big gyms, where compensation plans change and others control the money they make. Many times, they don't have an opportunity to move up in the organization, so they attempt to open their own business.

What inevitably happens is vintage material straight out of *The E-Myth*. The personal trainer's thoughts are: since I'm a good personal trainer or coach, I can open a good fitness business. The talents required for both endeavors are not the same—not by a long stretch.

New fitness business owners often don't anticipate the specifics they need to be aware of when opening a business. It starts with site selection. Most have no knowledge regarding commercial real estate, and have no idea where a business should be located, how much to pay per square foot, or how big their facility needs to be. All the mechanics of creating a model are foreign to them.

They know fitness. This one thing they know—and are experts at—can become a liability, because it's easy to focus on fitness while ignoring the business aspect.

I call these start-ups "micro-gyms." I am not referring here to the big-box chains like Gold's or Bally's. The micro-gyms are concepts like ours—small niche, personal training, CrossFit, or athlete conditioning gyms. Most of these businesses are built in bad locations (what I would call "C" locations), such as a warehouse with no visibility to customers, or a "bare bones" build-out with no showers or air conditioning. They have no brand to set them apart from others in the community, and no business plan from which to execute the model, add staff, grow the business, or add customer amenities.

KNOW HOW TO PRICE

Most problems begin at the price-setting level, because operators don't know how to properly price services. They undervalue their services and cut rates because they just want to get clients through the door. And, since they're not priced properly, they have a hard time adding staff and offering career opportunities. This dynamic keeps them stuck in the role of the producer. They can't get out of this vicious cycle—they can't focus on growing the business, because they're the ones conducting all the classes. They're the chief cook and bottle washer—doing all the marketing, administrative tasks, and coaching. The business sign has their name on it and when a client calls the number, it goes directly to the owner's cell phone. The business ends up being all about them.

Running an owner/operator business model almost inevitably leads to burnout. The one thing they love—training—becomes something they hate, because they're doing it 80 hours a week with no time off and no vacations. Eventually, they realize they are working for a boss who is a maniac ... *them*!

BUILDING IT AND HOPING THEY DON'T COME

I've mentioned the serious flaw in the big-box gym membership model of signing people up with the hope they will *not* come. The general fitness business mentality reflects the belief that 80 percent of members won't come, so they need to sign up as many people as possible, while planning to provide services for only 20 percent. In the micro-gym world, owners are focused on a smaller niche of clients because they have smaller facilities. Whether it takes the form of one-on-one, semi-private, or group training experiences, this training is "coach-based" versus "membership-based." The focus for these gyms becomes not only signing clients up, but also about retention and delivering results to keep clients around with the hopes they will continue to refer others to the gym.

But if the services are not priced properly, this point is never reached, because of lack of full-time staff to properly take care of clients. Again, ultimate responsibility falls on owners who are involved in a constant rat race of attempting to charge a higher rate than what clients could pay at a Gold's, Bally's, or a 24-Hour Fitness in order to make it all work.

Many look at the fitness business and think it's an easy and cheap business to enter because the facilities are not elaborate. There are no appliances to buy or large inventory investment, as in a restaurant start-up. Certainly, some equipment is required, and maybe showers and locker rooms need to be added. So they start the gym on a shoestring budget, which leads to everything from bad facilities, cheap rent, to no build-out. The business is underfunded and owners add equipment as they go or as volume dictates. They usually have no money-management skills—they haven't budgeted, created a pro forma, or developed a business plan.

Because of the lack of business sense and planning, there is no cash flow. Ultimately, failure results due to owners' optimism about what it's going to take to open the business, and the effort needed to ramp it up. They are unaware of the elements needed to break even or to eventually become profitable. Owners have to be focused on growing the business and taking all the necessary steps to get people in the door. If they do not have the capital or cash flow to build a great team to help accomplish this, it's not going to happen.

Incorrect pricing, building a gym around a successful coaching career, lack of business knowledge, and unrealistic expectations are common mistakes in the fitness industry. They eventually lead to burnout or a failed business. I'm not discounting the need to be great at what you do, or to be passionate about fitness. However, there is so much more to building a successful, repeatable, and profitable fitness business than just being a good coach. It takes more than simply opening a facility. It takes a well-thought-out plan that has been tested and proven repeatedly, resulting in a product that can be reproduced. Iron Tribe has figured out the specifics, documented them in our plan, and demonstrated the dynamics in our proven model.

CHAPTER 10

THE IRON TRIBE
ALTERNATIVE

"I want to franchise an Iron Tribe facility." Once someone gets to this point, how do we help him or her to realize that goal?

First, we have the multiple-step process of mutual evaluation to determine if we are the right fit for them, and if they are the right brand ambassadors for us. After watching an in-depth webinar on the business model, they are shown the capital requirements needed to open their business. We itemize where every dollar is to be spent: on build-out costs, equipment requirements, staff salaries, and beginning inventory. We lay out the operating capital they should have on hand. On top of that, we provide a business plan with tools to build a pro forma, which provides a schedule of getting their store to the break-even point, and eventually to a profitable level.

This plan is not theoretical. It's not something we hope will work. We've accomplished the end result ourselves, six times now.

We *know* how it works and we *know* how to make the business work for others.

Initially, some potential investors are surprised at the money required in opening a store, and the amount we charge the client for membership. One of the main reasons for the expense is the necessity for full-time staff, with two coaches per class. This part of our model is an incalculable asset to our members, and one of the primary reasons they keep coming back. Our staff *is* our brand—it's not a commodity, like a cup of coffee. We offer a high-level interaction with expert staff each and every day. This interaction depends on the involvement of great "A-player" team members. Finding and hiring the right staff is spelled out systematically: how to attract top-notch and talented people who are looking for a career, and how to give opportunity to team members. All these elements are built into a sophisticated business plan.

In order to grow a business, the owners must be involved in doing the right things. If they've been in the fitness industry in the past, they have operated as the product expert—the coach—and may not know how to make the transition to business owner (as with my story). We free them up from this primary responsibility and give them the necessary tools so they know exactly what to do with their time.

IT TAKES A TEAM AND WE ARE THE TEAM

Iron Tribe is an operations-based culture, and I am passionate about keeping it that way. We execute the same model we are selling, supporting, and reproducing. We understand everything about the business and how to improve it. We test every element before handing it down to others to emulate. Just like a football team has many players but only one main coach, the franchisees look to us, the franchisor, to provide leadership. We develop and call the plays, but we need the players to carry them out and complete the team.

Once the franchise business is up and running, our proprietary software tracks all their key performance indicators. We can evaluate what is going on inside the business very objectively. Are the behaviors being performed correctly? Is the business generating the estimated number of leads? Are they within the appropriate percentage of converting leads to consults? Are they within the appropriate percentage of converting consults to sales? These three elements require different support functions, and we address them all.

If the business is not getting enough leads, but has good sales numbers, then it is struggling at marketing. We peel back the layers to look at the amount spent on marketing and the specific mediums and campaigns being used. For instance, something as simple as having the phone answered correctly can separate a winning store from one that is a complete loser. If they are falling down in that aspect, we write a prescription of revisiting the phone and walk-in scripts, watching the associated videos on our franchisee website, or role-playing with one of our support reps. The issue can immediately be addressed and, as a result, turn the business around.

If phone calls are not being converted to consults, we know they are getting leads but not following up with an appropriate step. So we look at their dialog, the consultation process, and how they position the program. If they're getting leads but the leads are not resulting in sales, then we analyze the sales process and make sure they're sticking to the script. Once again, we prescribe an answer: revisit the consultation script, watch the associated videos, and practice role-playing with our reps, all of whom have store operations experience. Every type of metric we track drives a specific function of the business. By performing a full audit on the business, sending out a support rep, and addressing weaknesses, we can prescribe focused solutions to increase performance.

CAPITAL REQUIREMENTS

A potential franchisee usually asks up front, "What's it going to cost?" The amount will vary slightly from one region to another, due to variables such as construction costs, but the answer is somewhere between $275,000 and $350,000.

We are an approved Small Business Administration (SBA) company, which means we can accelerate the SBA process for those interested in that type of financing. But right now we don't offer direct financing ourselves, or any assistance to that end. It works out, actually, as part of our screening process. If people can't get access to that amount of capital, typically it's not going to be a good fit.

One of the biggest surprises in this model has been the number of investors who want to be partnered with fitness experts as the operators. We have experienced great success by playing matchmaker and combining those who have the resources to invest with those who have the passion and desire to execute and operate the model.

Our greatest strength is in knowing the model intimately and being able to direct franchisees by telling them what to do and when to do it. We know what our stores average in terms of new members a month, attrition rate, the percentage of members who renew, profit margins, cash on cash return, return on investment—all of the essential indicators in planning a business. We reveal all of this information in our franchise disclosure document, which also includes an earnings disclaimer.

This disclaimer provides the key numbers a franchisee needs in order to build a pro forma. We don't build it for them, at least not before they purchase. After purchase they can do a one-, two-, and three-year forecast based on our model, which enables them to plan for needs and cash flow. This forecast estimates the approximate expectation for return on capital, as well as a timeline for profit building within their business. Ordinarily, this kind of knowledge in the start-up of a new business is guesswork.

It's not guesswork with us.

SITE SELECTION: LOCATION, LOCATION, LOCATION

Our system addresses site selection, the entire lease negotiation process, and even the area of construction management. Many times, businesses get sideways in this tricky component of the construction process. They end up spending additional resources and, more often than not, additional time not allocated in the budget. By the time they open, they're out of operating capital. They start out behind the eight ball from the get-go. We designed a process that ensured this didn't happen.

The correct site selection is paramount. We have specific criteria for site requirements: the type of demographics it must have, daytime population of an area, the number of square feet in a location, and ceiling height required for ropes and rings. We ask, "Is there plenty of running space outside? Is there enough parking?" And finally, "Does this facility meet our criteria?" The checklist makes the process easy.

Once we have viable options, we negotiate several at a time. We have the ability to create leverage with the landlords, and we attempt to make the best possible decision at the end of the day. We try not to get emotionally tied to one building and end up overpaying for the facility. By considering only one spot and negotiating it for several months, there is a risk of having the deal fall apart. Then, the franchisee is way behind schedule and has to start all over. Our lease negotiation process lays out all the steps in successfully choosing the site, writing a letter of intent, and reviewing the lease. Our ultimate goal is properly executing a lease and, in the process, ending up with a great deal.

There are many tricky items on a lease agreement an owner needs to be aware of: personal guarantees, terms, and acceleration of rent upon renewal. It is important to remember to negotiate a renewal option, which guarantees an ability to renew. It is devastating to discover, at the end of the initial term, there is no way to renew the lease, and as a result, get booted out of the space.

We also evaluate the pros and cons of purchasing versus leasing the building. It does require higher net worth to purchase, but it makes a lot of sense to purchase if this is at all possible. Then, two businesses are built at once—value develops in real estate, as well as in the business. We have certainly taken advantage of this option in Birmingham. I currently own four of the six properties on which we operate our gyms. Our experience over the years has enabled us to lay out all the pros and cons of each requirement, and to direct others through the process step by step.

UNDER CONSTRUCTION

Once the franchisee signs the lease, we provide weekly steps to complete the process of developing a store and bringing it to completion. These steps include computer-aided drafting (CAD) designs, lay out for functionality of the space, and standardized equipment packages. To contemplate the flow and functionality of the space, we sketch in each design element. This not only provides a great visual, but also enables the franchisee to estimate the accurate build-out quote and understand how long the process should take.

The entire system of lease negotiation, architectural plans, and construction management has been developed through the process of opening our own stores, as well as multiple franchisee stores. We realize that most of our owners have never before owned a business and have not had the opportunity to oversee the construction process. We don't expect them to be experts in that area—we want them to be experts in opening and executing a successful business model! We manage all the necessary processes so they can concentrate on their modules in our proprietary training system, ITFU (Iron Tribe Fitness University). The franchisees spend the months prior to opening their store training within the system in our Birmingham stores. While here, they gain valuable experience while we oversee their construction process, and take it all the way to the final step of receiving the certificate of occupancy.

Is building a fitness business so simple that anyone with passion for it can accomplish it on their own? I think not. When an owner attempts to be a lone ranger and develop all the components from the beginning vision to the final product, the roadblocks and learning curve is intense. There are many opportunities to get sidetracked and make mistakes. Instead, with Iron Tribe, the experts who have already worked out the kinks provide all the steps, along with tutorials and involvement. For franchisees, there is a terrific synergy in having a team surrounding them—a team who has perfected the plan and executed it multiple times. This frees them up from tremendous start-up stress, enabling them to focus on their business.

To see some examples of our gyms and the finished product from the right site selection, lease negotiations, and construction management, go to **www.irontribefranchise.com/book.**

THE LEARNING CURVE: MINE AND YOURS

What have I learned about myself through my love affair with fitness? I discovered I love seeing people transform their bodies through fitness. And, if I'm not directly tied to that in some way, shape, or fashion, then I don't feel fulfilled. I have determined the lifelong pursuit I want to develop with excellence. I believe everyone has a God-given ability to excel in at least one area, and through this gifting, they are able to contribute to others around him or her. Our responsibility is to find that area of excellence and then channel all our energy and passion into that one thing.

In my experience, I've found that most people seem to be content with mediocrity in their vocation. They don't take the time or energy required to become a master of their craft. This creates a problem, and I have fallen into it—being mediocre results in a lack of self-respect and positive self-concept, which is vital in achieving success, accomplishment, and personal satisfaction.

Not pursuing excellence has a negative effect on relationships, health, energy, stress, and just about everything else. If we are not pursuing excellence, not pouring all our energy and passion into something significant, then every morning our reflection in the mirror reveals mediocrity, at best. I think it's impossible to fully like and value oneself unless we know we are pursuing excellence in at least one worthy endeavor.

I think we can only become excellent at doing the things we love to do. When I was working out in my garage and realized it was the best part of my day, I began laying the groundwork for starting over and making that feeling part of my job. I wanted to do it with excellence. I wanted to build a team and give people career opportunities in an industry where this wasn't happening.

For me, passion drove it all. It *was* a huge risk to start over, but I followed my heart and that has resulted in an incredible amount of renewed energy, self-confidence, and an assurance that I'm doing exactly what I'm supposed to be doing. This is what God intended for me, and the talents and resources He gave me are being used to help others.

Making the decision to pursue my passion by knowing what I love to do, and pouring all my energy and effort into the pursuit of excellence, has given me an incredible lifestyle. I've been able to build a profitable business, one that is centered on other people. Iron Tribe presents amazing growth opportunities for my staff, and raises thousands of dollars for charity partners every year.

A big part of the payoff has been the ability to mentor guys like Tra, Richard, and Jim. They have already exceeded their wildest dreams by owning their own business or partnering with me. In Tra Griffin's case, he has excelled by overseeing six of our stores. Believing in these guys, teaching them everything I know, and learning from their area of expertise has been very rewarding. We have been able to systemize a great business and build something bigger than ourselves.

At the core of Iron Tribe, the focus is the customer. We continue to build value for the customer and never lose sight of this goal. The results have been the creation of a dynamic business that has an impact on our world; helping people while making money. It has also given me great freedom in my schedule. If I need to take time away for other pursuits, I have a dedicated team in place that can execute the business in my absence. I can choose to work as much or as little as I want. Of course, I still work a full schedule—not because I have to, but because I love it!

This year, I plan to take a week off to travel to India to visit the water wells established last year. I will be able to take an additional three or four weeks off for vacation with my family. Ultimately, my schedule comes down to life on my terms—making sure I'm creating value for others, but also investing in my wife, kids, church, and all the things that are important to me.

YOU, OUR NEXT FRANCHISEE?

If this story of rapid growth centered on passion for fitness, service, and detailed systemization has appealed to you, then you may be someone we want to talk with! We are always looking for good franchise partners who want to join us in replicating our brand promise for more people.

In the franchising world, when talking about the where, what, when, and who, the *who* is the most important part. If we get the right person on our team, one who is passionate about our service and embraces our core values, then we know we can be successful together. We have built a model that works, and are looking for others who are ready to execute it. The worst thing we could do is to bring the wrong person into the equation.

That is why we spend so much time profiling candidates in order to find the best coaches, the best managers, and the best operators. We use personality profiles such as the Kolbe test and the Myers Briggs analysis. We've designed a hiring package that pinpoints the kind of people we are looking for—the ones we want to be a part of our program. We are constantly looking for potential hires and franchisees who share our core values and who mesh with our business practices—those who desire to be successful along with us.

If you have read this far and are interested in joining us, ask yourself some questions. "Does this sound like something I would be interested in? Would I be a good fit for this team? Are they a good fit for me? Do we share similar values and work ethic?" This is the most important process before looking at the where, when, and what. *It's the who.*

If you are right for this system, together we can impact the world and deliver life-changing fitness. We want to partner with you to build another incredible fitness community in your city, with your very own Iron Tribe Fitness gym! I look forward to meeting one day to discuss the growth opportunity with *you*!

Could you be the Next Success Story?

THE IRON TRIBE
FITNESS FRANCHISE

TURN-KEY BUSINESS OPPORTUNITY

FREE

OVER $799 VALUE COLLECTION OF 3 DVDS

PLUS OTHER RESOURCES—

FOR A LIMITED TIME

Got a passion for fitness? Want to turn that passion into profits?

If so, you may qualify to own the <u>ultimate</u> lifestyle business—as an Iron Tribe Fitness franchisee. We've gone from a 400-sq-ft garage to more than 50 units across America in 3 years. What's the secret? Our turn-key systems ensure your success by giving you a clear, proven path to follow:

- Predictable Income, with plug-and-play systems for lead generation, new customer acquisition, and multiple recurring revenue streams. Prospects are pre-determined to join before you ever speak to them!

- Market Researched and Protected Territories, so you can build your business and forget about competition.

- Done-For-You Equipment and Construction Packages, to help you ramp up to profitability fast!

To learn more about the Iron Tribe Franchising opportunity, please complete and return the form below for your FREE Gift. You'll receive a 3-DVD Collection of videos documenting the 11 Essential Systems of the ITF business model, location tours, marketing campaigns that pull in clients by the boatload, and a whole lot more. The value of this DVD training is $799, but it's being offered FREE to the first qualified person in your area. After your area is taken, this offer is void and must be withdrawn without notice.

PLEASE PRINT CLEARLY TO GUARANTEE THE DELIVERY OF YOUR FREE DVD COLLECTION:

Your Name: _____

Business Name: _____

Mailing Address: _____

_____

City: _____   State: _____

Zip: _____

Phone: (_____) _____

Fax: (_____) _____

Email: _____
(*we do NOT believe in Spam*)

Are you a trainer or micro-gym owner currently?

_____

What are your top 3 locations choices (zips codes) for your ITF Franchise? _____

What is your biggest stumbling block in your business at the moment? (This is confidential, so please be honest):

_____

_____

_____

Your Signature *(Required)*: _____

Date: _____

Submitting this form constitutes permission for us to contact you regarding these interests via mail, email, fax, phone and other devices in the future.

4 EASY WAYS TO CLAIM YOUR FREE
$799 DVD COLLECTION:

1. Scan and Email this form to: Kelli@IronTribeFranchise.com

2. Fax this form back to 1-205-226-8676

3. Call the Office toll free at 1-855-226-8699

4. Visit www.IronTribeFranchise.com and fill out the online form

How can you use this book?

MOTIVATE

EDUCATE

THANK

INSPIRE

PROMOTE

CONNECT

Why have a custom version of *Iron Tribe*?

- Build personal bonds with customers, prospects, employees, donors, and key constituencies
- Develop a long-lasting reminder of your event, milestone, or celebration
- Provide a keepsake that inspires change in behavior and change in lives
- Deliver the ultimate "thank you" gift that remains on coffee tables and bookshelves
- Generate the "wow" factor

Books are thoughtful gifts that provide a genuine sentiment that other promotional items cannot express. They promote employee discussions and interaction, reinforce an event's meaning or location, and they make a lasting impression. Use your book to say "Thank You" and show people that you care.

Iron Tribe is available in bulk quantities and in customized versions at special discounts for corporate, institutional, and educational purposes. To learn more please contact our Special Sales team at:

1.866.775.1696 • sales@advantageww.com • www.AdvantageSpecialSales.com